RETHINKING
THE
CHRISTIAN MESSAGE

RETHINKING

THE

CHRISTIAN

MESSAGE

BY

W. NORMAN PITTENGER

GREENWICH · CONNECTICUT · 1956

© 1956 BY THE SEABURY PRESS, INCORPORATED

LIBRARY OF CONGRESS CATALOG CARD NUMBER: 56-7972

DESIGNED BY P. ATKINSON DYMOCK

PRINTED IN THE UNITED STATES OF AMERICA

IN MEMORY

OF

FLORENCE HICKSON FORRESTER

AND IN

AFFECTIONATE GRATITUDE

TO

DONALD FRASER FORRESTER

PREFACE

INVITATIONS TO deliver a course of lectures at the School of the Prophets in San Francisco, California, and later to the clergy of the Diocese of Olympia, seemed to provide an opportunity to think through some of the major Christian apologetic problems of our day. The lectures, duly delivered before a friendly, if critical, company of clergy, are here presented to a wider audience, with some omissions and with considerable expansion.

It is obvious that in a few chapters one cannot cover the whole subject of Christian thought in our time. I have tried to give attention to several particular matters which seem to me of crucial importance. My main interest has not been in cultural and sociological factors which bear upon the presentation of Christianity—I have sought to do this in another book, *The Historic Faith and a Changing World*. My concern has been with intellectual difficulties created for our contemporaries by certain ways of stating the Christian message. I hope that I have not forgotten the vital quality of Christian truth and its necessary implementation in Christian living.

The informed reader will find in these chapters traces

of the influence of Rudolf Bultmann's "de-mythologiz-ing," not so much in an acceptance of Bultmann's answer to the problem but in his vivid statement of it. I acknowledge but do not regret this fact. Since the lectures were "popular," in being addressed to parish clergymen rather than theological experts, I did not think it necessary or desirable to discuss this question at the length which it deserves. My own standpoint will be sufficiently clear, I trust, from what I have said in a more popular vein.

An Anglican who accepts the essential affirmations of historical Christianity, but who also believes that one of our necessary contemporary tasks is the re-thinking, re-interpreting, re-stating, of these essentials in the light of the best knowledge of the times, cannot but face the criticism that he is "watering-down" the faith. It all depends upon what one means by "the faith." If it is a set of propositions, that is one thing; if it is a response to the movement of God to men, culminating in response to the fact of Christ, that is something else again. I for one do not believe that the notion that newer knowledge, in biblical criticism, science, modern philosophical thought, has left the Christian message entirely untouched is a notion which can really be defended; on the other hand, it is my conviction that the popular "return to orthodoxy" is often to be identified with a failure of nerve and a refusal to face the inevitable.

I am indebted to my friends, the Right Reverend Karl Morgan Block, Bishop of California, and the Right

Reverend Stephen Fielding Bayne, Bishop of Olympia, for the first invitation to give these lectures; and to the Reverend Canon Eric Montizambert, Warden of the School of the Prophets, for his gracious hospitality while I was a visitor at that valuable institution in San Francisco. I am also grateful to the clergy who heard the lectures both at the School of the Prophets and at the Olympia Clergy Conference, for their courteous attention and friendly interest.

To the main body of this book I have ventured to add, by way of introduction, my inaugural lecture as Charles Lewis Gomph Professor of Christian Apologetics at the General Theological Seminary. I think that this chapter will indicate, in a more general way, what seems to me the necessary approach to a Christian apologetic in our time.

W. NORMAN PITTENGER

CONTENTS

RETHINKING

THE

CHRISTIAN MESSAGE

I

CHRISTIAN APOLOGETICS

THE enterprise of Christian apologetics has often been
criticized. Sometimes this is because the word "apologetics" suggests, for those whose Latin is weak, an effort
to hold the fort when all chance of victory by offensive
action is lost. But the Latin word itself comes close to
meaning "reasonable justification"; and if it is defense at
all, it is defense in a way very different from the whispered
and timid apology of popular thought. It is defense in
a bold and daring manner, in the sure confidence that
Christianity can meet and overcome opposition because
in it is the very truth of God Himself. Sometimes, and
more particularly by certain theologians of our own
times, apologetics has been derided or denounced because
it is felt to be an attempt to build up a case for our
faith on grounds that are ultimately secular or human-

istic—*merely* philosophical, *purely* natural. This is the attack of men like Karl Barth, who regard any such enterprise as both blasphemous and absurd. Of course, we must concede (unless we subscribe to what for many of us is the impossible position of the Vatican Council of 1870) at least part of their point—namely, that we cannot, from the human side alone, without divine grace, reach to the eternal God. Yet we must at the same time insist that the God whom we worship, and by whom we have been given newness of life in Christ Jesus, is the God of cosmic order, of right reason, of ultimate truth; and therefore it is unthinkable for us that the effort to state what reason we have for our Christian position is bound to be a meaningless and fruitless labour, with which God is not pleased. Despite our sin, God is in our understanding, chastened as we must be in our trust in its deliverances.

But the erroneous extreme of the Barthian attack ought to make us conscious of two facts: one, that Christian apologetics is not simply another name for ordinary philosophy of religion; and second, that it is only from within the household of faith that we can speak as apologists, and then always with that humility which becomes those whose speaking is of the ineffable mystery of God and His ways with men.

1

Those who have read the Apologists, those early Greek and Latin Christians who sought to present Christianity to the Graeco-Roman world of the first few centuries of the Christian era, will recall that they had three great objectives. First, the negative one of forcing their hearers to a rejection of idolatry, to turn "to the living God from dead idols"; second, and as a consequence, the positive objective of proclaiming the existence of the one true God; and third, the central affirmation—which some of them reached only by intimation, so busy were they on the earlier levels—of the truth of God's revelation to, and redemption of, the world in Jesus Christ. Classically, in Origen's great *Contra Celsum,* this threefold task is set forth; and nearly a century later, in Lactantius for instance, we find the same intent implicit.

I have no intention of minimizing the long period of Christian thought between these apologists and our own day. But in our own day, when once more we who are Christians confront a pagan world, our task can rightly be said to be exactly the same as theirs. First of all, we must show, with all the clarity cast by the light of the Gospel, the idolatry of our time—its setting up of nationalism, racism, vulgar materialism, the "bitch-goddess" success, communism, yes, and Americanism too, as if they were exhaustive and adequate expressions of the meaning of human existence. We must overthrow them. But, second, we cannot stop with this destructive work. We must proclaim, unfalteringly, and show (so far as this can be done), by all the devices and arguments at our disposal, that it is only in the one true and living God, the God of the Jewish people, the God of the Prophets, who is the God and Father of all men, that life can be given significance and purpose. And we must claim the whole world as His world, a world which the worship of idols distorts and perverts, but which the recognition of the true God restores to its right dignity and order. And thirdly and most important, we must declare the Gospel of God in Christ, the faith in the incarnate and redeeming Lord in His Holy Church, as that which alone can bring final purpose to our human existence and empower men to live as men in a world where under present conditions they are almost forced to live as sophisticated yet frustrated beasts. But we can do the first two of these things, in a fashion which is proper for *Christian* apologists, only if we are ourselves committed to the last of them.

2

The task of Christian apologetics is a *churchly* task, as the discipline itself is a churchly discipline. By this I mean that we who seek to defend the faith must always be those who, in giving a reason, are believing men, men of the Church, participants in the life of the divine community for whose faith we would speak. It is not our duty, on the basis of a world understood entirely apart from God's mighty act in Christ and in the Church which is bearer of and witness to that act, to construct a world view which will perhaps admit the possibility of some such theism as Christianity assumes and, therefore, will perhaps admit the further possibility of the Christian position itself. It is our task and joy to see the whole world, and all of life, in the light of our major commitment. It is our privilege to interpret the whole world, and all of life, in terms of the central affirmation of God in Christ for man's wholeness. It is our obligation to claim, in consequence of this affirmation, that the God whom we know and adore in the incarnate and redeeming Lord, in His Body the Holy Church, is the Lord also of the whole world and of all life. We have a position; we start from there. In a profound sense, then, it is true that the best apologetic *for* Christianity is a compelling statement *of* it.

But there is more than that. For we are to seek to commend this faith, this worship, this engraced life in Christ, to a non-believing world. It is, therefore, our duty to find ways of stating the Christian position as winningly, as attractively, as we can. In so doing, we must remember the distinction between peripheral and essential, lest we clutter the faith with irrelevancies that can be a needless cause of stumbling to many; we must remember, with Erasmus, that the articles of faith must be as few as are necessary to the facts; we must remember, above all, that we do not have all the answers, since we talk of a great mystery which no man can fully know, no mind completely fathom. And in this seeking to commend, it is our great responsibility to find words, phrases, and an idiom, which do not present

7

semantic difficulties to those whom we would win. For is it not true that much, although not most, of our trouble today is that the words which for us within the great tradition are richly significant, are for those without often meaningless babble or offensive chatter? Yet the Christian faith is not in *words,* but in the power of God; and it is incumbent upon us to discover the ways of stating that power which will open men's minds and win men's hearts, and so bring them into captivity to the obedience of Christ.

3

What are the qualities of spirit which must mark him who would be an apologist for Christianity? First of all, we must be men of strong conviction. We must know whom we have believed; we must be persuaded that He is able to keep and to do that which He has promised. The way to such conviction is simply the way of Christian discipleship—the way of prayer, of sacramental life, of meditation on the Scriptures, of dedication and perseverance in our course. But the way to such conviction is also an intellectual way; we must know the faith, know it through study and thought, know it so deeply and so well that we know it not with our minds alone but in the whole of our being.

Secondly, we who would be apologists for Christianity must be men of humility. Not only is the Gospel of God greater than our little minds, but we must ever think and talk as those who know this to be the fact.

The limitless ocean of God's being, the amazing depths of human personality, the strange and wonderful ways of relationship between man and man, and between God and man—here are areas of life and experience of which we may speak only with the hesitation born of humble recognition, yet with the genuine conviction born of faith. The light which is Christ shineth, but we dare not forget that it shineth "in darkness." Much we do not know, much we can never know. We must accept that fact, and the further fact that every man to whom we talk is a mystery, into whose secret heart we can never enter, whose inner life we must reverence as a place where God dwells. So we can never seek to manipulate men, twist them to our ways of thinking, cheat them in argument, or coerce them by some wrong pressure, intellectual or even personal. We must commend the faith through that humility of spirit, as through that integrity of mind and honesty of argument, which alone can reflect something of the mystery of Truth in a world great beyond our seeing.

Finally, we must be men of sensitivity, of generosity, of charity. The eternal reality of God is a goodness ever diffusive of itself: so we read in the Angelic Doctor. We, who are little and derived creatures, must reflect something of that overflowing charity, that boundless generosity. We must be sensitive to the widest reaches of the divine self-disclosure. God speaks in many places, but *not* always in specifically religious terms—as O. C. Quick said, "God works in many an unrecognized Bethlehem and Calvary." He works outside the Holy Catholic Church, difficult as it seems for some of us, evidently, to recognize the fact. And although we must be ready to "show up" the pretensions of "worldly wisdom," we must also remember that our God is the God by whom all things were made through His Eternal Word. That Word is incarnate for us men in Christ, but He is at work *everywhere* in divers portions, in partial revelations and adumbrated redemption. He is met in response, everywhere, by the Holy Spirit, who everywhere presses the creation home to God, by the Spirit who is the great and everlasting Amen through created things to the God who created them, even though He be uniquely known in the holy community which is marked by His "fellowship." Generosity of spirit in recognizing and accepting these facts will make a world of difference in our way of being apologists.

And as to other men whom we would win—other Christians and non-Christians—can we fail to be in charity towards them, loving them because God made them, because God loves them, because God keeps them, because God has bought them, and all men, with the precious blood of our Saviour? If we are Christian, we dare not be bitter in spirit towards any brother for whom Christ died. Rather, we must seek, in all humility but with all love, to win him to the saving Lord in His Holy Church, remembering that we too are sinners, we too are blind, we too are weak, yet thankful that God has called us out of darkness into His marvellous light, graciously willing to unite us in His Son's mystical Body with that Son of His love and so to call us by His name. Often enough, it will not be by word said, but by charity shown, that we shall most effectively commend the Gospel of God in Christ, most certainly win others to faithful membership in Christ's mystical Body. And this is why our apologetic must be ecumenical in spirit, as the word goes, willing to learn and willing to share with all who profess and call themselves Christian, even while we remain loyal sons of *Ecclesia Anglicana,* Catholic and reformed, and are prepared vigorously to defend the doctrine, discipline, and worship of Christ's Holy Catholic Church as this Church has received and maintains the same.

II

I suppose that we should all agree that the Christian Church is not making the impact which it should and could make upon the life and thought of the men and women of our time. To say this is to state a platitude. Any parish priest would confirm the truth of the assertion; and most of us, whether in parish or in seminary or in other areas of the Church's work, have a deep concern about the problem. We know the Church's Gospel and its life in grace to be a vital necessity for men; we wish to make that Gospel and that life as compelling and as attractive as we can; we feel that somehow great numbers of people do not respond as they might. And we are worried about it.

But in much of our thinking upon this all-important subject, we have tended to place all or most of the blame for the situation upon those who reject the message of the Church or refuse to listen to it with attention and interest. We are not so likely to give time and attention to possible defects, if I may use the word, in the message as we present it, or in the particular methods which have been used in that presentation.

I make this comment advisedly, for we are told often enough that the Church has expended much effort in "accommodating" itself to modern ways, and that it is precisely this attempted accommodation which is the reason that the Christian message has seemed irrelevant or insignificant. What has happened, it is said, is that Christianity has been so "watered down," so adjusted to contemporary culture and thought, that it has lost its cutting-edge and has become nothing more than a republication of ordinary, elevated moral and religious sentiments. Now there is, of course, a sense in which this is true. There was a time, not so long since, when certain varieties of "liberalism" seemed intent on twisting the Christian Gospel so that it became in effect nothing but the ideas of all men of good-will. It became, too often, not a Gospel, not Good News, but the restatement of "natural morality" and "natural religion." And it is in reaction from this perverse tendency to destroy the imperative of the Gospel as real news to needy men that we have seen the rise of the newer orthodoxies of our day, with their vigorous reassertion of the sinfulness of man, his need for redemption, the Christian message as one of saving grace, the imperfection of men even when redeemed, and all the rest of the stock-in-trade of modern theological discussion.

But it still remains true that there is a kind of "offense" in much of our presentation of Christianity which is neither integral to the central assertions of the Christian message itself, nor necessary in making its imperatives vivid and compelling to modern men. Sometimes we seem to have been ready to assume that because Christianity must indeed be a "scandal" to worldly people, must make demands which men are not usually ready to answer easily and glibly, must involve a complete turn-about in our ordinary ways of thinking and living, it must therefore be presented in as "offensive" a manner as possible. By this I do not mean, of course, that we think that it must be presented disagreeably. Rather I mean that we tend increasingly to feel that because our familiar words, conventionally traditional theological ideas, and habitual modes of presentation of Christian truth do not seem to make much sense to the majority of our contemporaries, we take it for granted that the trouble is all with our contemporaries and not very much with us. So we devise schemes by which we can at least say the same things, but in "attractive" ways, without going to the trouble of penetrating into the actual difficulties in the old theological formulations and their presentation which may be the basic reason for the acknowledged fact that our contemporaries do not seem to make much sense of Christianity as they hear it, read about it, and understand (or fail to understand) what it is all about.

1

Whenever I hear a speaker at some large ecclesiastical gathering tell his audience that what is needed today is "definite Church teaching," I groan inwardly. For I know perfectly well what is likely to be the meaning of this assertion. If only we will more assiduously repeat the traditional phrases, perhaps explaining a little here and there; if only we will intensify our affirmations of "what the Church has always said"; if only we will return to the "biblical theology" which is the basis for our Christian preaching, all will be well. That is what is usually meant. But I know perfectly well, too, that such a procedure will have very little affect upon those whom we wish to win to the Church; and, indeed, very little affect upon those who are already with us but who are sorely in need of a deeper understanding of the meaning of the Christian message to which they give tacit and uninformed consent.

Recently I was speaking at a meeting of young adults concerned with a consideration of the meaning of the Christian moral standard in our day. After my address, an older member of the group said that he felt that the solution of our difficulty in making Christianity significant to contemporary men and women was "the reassertion of the authority of the priesthood." And when I suggested that in itself this would do very little for anybody, but that the real solution was the bringing of Christianity into the actual situations where men are in doubt and despair about the value of life, and in those situations pointing to the Christian interpretation of life without regard to our invaluable traditional formulations, the gentleman expressed his awful fear that such a procedure would result in grave damage to the faith which must necessarily be reduced to a mere moralism in that endeavour. This incident seems to me to symbolize what is wrong with so much of our thinking on these matters.

In the first place, it shows the implicit notion that authoritative statement is our prime need, as if loud and blustering assertions carry any real weight with thoughtful people. In the second place, it shows an unwillingness to run the risk of exposing Christian teaching to the winds of modern thought and experience. And in the third place, it shows a fear that Christianity cannot be restated without being completely negated. Such "faithless fears" seem to me to indicate that those who share my questioner's point of view are really at bottom not too sure of the integrity of Christianity itself. They are believers whose fundamental attitude is doubt and scepticism.

The truth is that our message simply does not "get across." And the truth is also that when some real effort is made to "get it across" in understandable language and with the use of contemporary idiom, it meets a ready and glad response. The Department of Christian Education of the National Council of the Episcopal Church has been seeking to educate first the clergy and then the laity in the actual problems which men and women today must face, showing the way in which the Gospel meets them where they are and helps them make sense of their experience. *The Church's Teaching* series, and similar projects in other denominations, are concerned to do precisely this; and the fact that they have had a surprisingly cordial reception is an indication both of a real need and of the hearty welcome to any attempt to meet that need.

But I for one should wish to go further. I am convinced that there are difficulties much more basic than the problem of relevance—a problem which the Church is slowly learning to meet. The difficulties to which I refer are in the realms first of semantics, or the meaning of words, and second of what I should call "forms of thought." I believe that the Church generally is not yet meeting these difficulties in anything like as earnest and serious a way as the situation demands. Let me say something about each area, very briefly at this time, for I shall be dealing with aspects of them in the later chapters of this book.

2

The problem of semantics is simply the problem of words and phrases, and of the meaning that they have for those who use them or hear them. In our own day, for reasons into which it would be interesting to enter but for which we do not have time in this place, the language which is conventional in the Christian Church seems to have very little significance for the average man or woman. Or, when the language does have some significance, very often that significance bears slight relation to the historically valid denotation or connotation of the phrases. Words like Incarnation, Atonement, Redemption, Sin, Justification, Sanctification, and the like have lost for our contemporaries, unless they are within the charmed circle of informed theological understanding (and sometimes not even then), that wealth of association which, to Christians of another day, gave them richness and value of a high degree. These men and women of our day do not know what we are talking about when we use terms like these. And their ignorance is so deep, their capacity for understanding so slight, that even when we attempt to explain this or that phrase, the illumination is only for the moment. Anyone who has sought to teach in a popular "school of religion" will testify that this is the fact even among active churchgoers.

Presently I shall have occasion to emphasize the value of the traditional language, which has about it that "power" which Professor Paul Tillich has shown to attach to words that have long traditional religious worth. The language is, indeed, often "numinous" in quality. But at the moment I wish simply to emphasize the other side of the truth: words like this can as easily be barriers to meaning as conveyers of meaning, and even for those who habitually use them and think they understand them they can be like the blessed word "Mesopotamia," producing the right emotion but entirely without significant content. If we hope to bring people into the Christian community and enable them to share the life which is made available in that community, we must somehow learn, as one of my revered teachers used to say, to "put it in other words."

3

The other area to which I have referred is that of "forms of thought." I have chosen this phrase to express a kind, or way, of thinking, a mode of approach to life's exigent demands, a set of mind which prevails in a given generation or a particular milieu. It is not only that our actual words, phrases, language, have very little meaning for our contemporaries; it is also that our whole way of thinking, our set of mind, seems to them to have no relationship to the way of thinking, the set of mind that is familiar to them and in terms of which their ordinary life must be lived.

I shall hope to illustrate this difficulty in later chapters, but for the moment I wish only to insist that men and women today not only fail often to understand what we are saying, but also cannot comprehend the way in which we think—to them the whole framework of our thought is alien to their experience. Our presuppositions are different from theirs, as is also our structure of thought. Hence we do not have any vital point of contact with them, and whatever we may say will seem remote and unreal.

No Christian, certainly, would wish to assert that *all* of the presuppositions and the total structure of thinking of modern people can be right. Indeed, we should wish to say that many of their presuppositions and much in their structure of thinking must be recognized as quite false and in need of drastic correction. There is no real depth, no adequate discernment of the tragic dimension of man's existence, no sufficient understanding of the "beyond" which is also within. Yet it may be the case that, in certain respects, modern men and women are not altogether in the wrong. It may be that they have learned truths from what we are too prone to call "secular" sources, that are genuine truths, truths of which Christians who believe that Truth is ultimately but a manifestation of God should be ready and willing to take account.

In fact one of the important points in the history of the Christian Church, to which our attention needs again and again to be directed, is that in the great ages of the faith, and among the notable leaders in the enterprise of Christian thought about God, the world, and man, it has been considered essential that the Christian message should be understood and presented in the light of the secular truth of the time. Clement of Alexandria and Origen, for instance, sought to do this with respect to the middle-Platonism of their day. Augustine was alert to the neo-Platonism which was prevalent in his time. Thomas Aquinas worked through the revived Aristotelianism of the thirteenth century and endeavoured to state Christianity in its idiom. English religious humanism, as represented by the wonderful school of which Erasmus, Thomas More, John Colet, John Fisher, and others were leaders, did the same with the new thought of their age. Here are instances—and only a few of the many which might be cited—which we should never forget. Of course, there was the danger of assimilating the distinctively biblical witness to some prevailing mode of thought, and none of the men mentioned was free from this danger. Yet failure to be keenly aware of, and refusal to present Christianity in terms derived from, the general forms of thought of a given historical era, have resulted over and over again in an ingrown and sterile theology and in a loss of vital contact with the men and women whom our Lord Jesus Christ came to save.

And when we are told, as we so often are told these days, that the Bible has its own distinctive *weltanschauung,* we must agree with the assertion but hasten to point out that this is different from a *weltbild;* the biblical view of the relation of God and man, of God and the creation, is not to be identified with the particular cosmology and the mythology which the writers of the sacred books necessarily held because it was conventional in their time. That same basic biblical view can be presented in a multitude of philosophical idioms, with recognition of many different scientific descriptions of the world process, and with much variation from generation to generation so far as prevailing cultural patterns are concerned. Historically this has certainly been the case.

I am convinced, then, that the fault is not all with our age and its ideas. And even if it were, it would seem to me to be the part of Christian honesty to examine oneself and one's own tradition most carefully, in an effort to determine how much of that fault may be the *indirect* result of some serious failure on our part. I am not at all sure that we are performing that task of self-examination as honestly and as rigorously as we should.

4

Our concern in this book is with the intellectual or theological side of the problems which I have indicated. Questions of a specifically sociological nature I must leave to those who are particularly competent to handle them. The wider cultural chasm between Christian thought and much of the life of our time I have sought to discuss elsewhere (in *The Historic Faith and a Changing World*). What we shall attempt in this book is a consideration of the relationship between the faith that lives at the heart of Christianity and the knowledge of our own day, including the scientific facts which are by now fairly ascertained and the philosophical implications of these facts which are already part of the mental furniture of the majority of thoughtful people. We shall consider the implications of these forms of thought for men's ways of looking at the world, and the difficulties which that knowledge, and its implications, create for the Christian teacher and preacher. Finally, we shall attempt a constructive statement of the essentials of Christian faith in the light of such knowledge, both scientific fact and philosophical implication, taking one or two specific Christian assertions as illustrative of the whole enterprise. As a preliminary to this, moreover, we shall have something to say about words and their meaning and indicate some of the serious problems that arise because our language within the Christian Church and the language ordinarily employed outside it seem to have little chance of meaningful encounter.

First of all, however, I wish to mention three areas where, as I think, Christianity seems to be in conflict with the general patterns of our day. I believe that these have not yet received sufficient attention from Christian thinkers. The first of these areas has to do with the vastness of the world as we have come to know it through modern scientific research in the realm of astrophysics and in the realm of microphysics. In contrast to this enormously expanded view of the world the Christian view seems to be utterly insignificant. The second area is in the realm of knowledge. Modern thinking insists on the relativity of all of our knowledge of truth and looks with suspicion on claims made by anyone to ultimate truth. But Christians assert some kind of "absolute" knowledge about God and His ways. The last area is concerned with the widely accepted contemporary definition of "nature" as the inclusive reality with which we have to deal, as contrasted with the Christian notion of a reality that is "supernatural" with which religion is presumed to be especially related. I should not claim that these are the only areas of conflict, but I should certainly say that among all the areas which one might mention these are peculiarly important ones.

5

Anyone who is acquainted with the vast literature which deals with the exploration of space, the wonders of the galaxies, and the almost endless time-series that these involve—and, at the popular level, with the expression of these themes in what is called "science-fiction"—must agree that the expanding of our notion of the sheer size of the universe, the possibilities now frequently discussed that there may be intelligent living beings of some kind on other planets elsewhere in the universe, the amazing prolongation of the time-series as modern science presents it, have had their inevitable affect on the thinking of modern men and women. And it is equally inevitable that men and women must wonder whether the Christian epic is not too small for such a tremendous world. It is doubtless true, as Pascal would tell us, that we do not really need to yield to "astronomical intimidation"; yet the average man or woman is either appalled or fascinated by these overwhelming new dimensions; and the Christian message, if it is to have meaning for such persons, must be presented in such terms that it does not appear too "teeny-weeny" for the illimitable spaces and the unimaginable time-span with which men are now familiar. As we shall see, many of the Christian attempts to meet this problem are either absurdly anthropocentric or lack the grand sweep and the cosmic perspective that is implicit in the ancient *Logos* theology.

Again, the emphasis which is laid in so much modern thought on the serious limitations of human knowledge, both methodologically and in result, cannot help but conflict with the kind of claim which many believe to be made by the Christian disciple and by the Church of which he is a member—the supposed claim that we are in possession of an absolute and ultimate truth which admits of no doubt or question. I am not saying that the Christian Church in fact claims this; indeed, I am sure that it does not. Certainly there is a sense in which the Christian must say, if he believes the Gospel to be true at all, that he knows the truth. But this does not necessarily mean, and ought never to be taken to mean, the kind of absolutism in knowledge which is often thought (not infrequently by theologians and preachers) to be asserted. "The light shineth in darkness"; "we know in part . . ." Yet it is surely true

26

that many of our contemporaries feel strongly the absurdity and pretense of any man having "the last word on everything." Oddly enough, the defender of Christianity often attempts to counter modern science by saying that many give to it the kind of infallibility that they deny to religious knowledge, assuming that science claims to speak with precisely the absoluteness that it criticizes in religion. But this is simply not true. Whatever may be the practical attitude of our contemporaries towards science, and however much they may cite scientific authority in a rather naive fashion, the leading men of science never make any such claims to absolute authority or infallible knowledge, and the average man is quite alert to the dubieties of the scientific world. Whatever trust he may have in science, he has very largely because science demonstrably "delivers the goods"; when religious faith shows that it too can "deliver the goods," though in a different way, with different techniques, and with different kinds of pragmatic proof, he may begin to have more trust in those who speak for it. In any event, contemporary philosophical thought, either in its instrumentalist phase with its reduction of truth to simple workability or in its positivistic phase with its dismissal of metaphysical, moral, and theological assertions as "nonsense," is insistent on the limitations of human knowledge and the necessity for a certain agnosticism about ultimate matters. To some of us, such a position has a close resemblance to the ways of true religion, but there are many theological experts and many more parish clergy who do not see this and would not allow it.

Finally, the concept of nature has been so developed in our time, especially by the so-called "new naturalists," that most of the old attacks by Christian apologists completely miss the mark. All too often these apologists set up as "nature" a straw-man in whom nobody has believed for nearly half-a-century; they have no difficulty in knocking him down, but they do not come any nearer to restoring confidence in Christian claims than before they began their manoeuvre. With nature now seen as including the moral, spiritual, and often the specifically religious values which were excluded from simple nineteenth century rationalistic and materialistic naturalism, many of our contemporaries who have read, for example, the writings of Irwin Edman or Paul Weiss, to mention only two names of those who have been popularizing the newer naturalism, do not see that there can be anything "above nature." The central religious meaning of the "supernatural" needs, therefore, to be stated in a different fashion, no longer as another storey added to the world but as a pervasive reality operative within the world. The other aspect of the "supernatural," often insisted upon by orthodox apologists, has to do with the miraculous, which for most moderns seems to introduce meaningless chaos into the whole order of things.

As in the earlier areas, the idea of the supernatural

need not be understood in such a fashion that it contradicts the natural order, nor need it deny whatever
residual significance the concept of the miraculous may
possess (whatever we may think of the sense of retain-
ing a word that is so loaded with unfortunate associations). It need not involve a series of catastrophic
interferences from outside (outside what, and from
where?) into the "more or less settled" process of creation. My point here is simply that the ordinary person
is not much helped towards accepting Christianity when
he hears the parson talk glibly about the supernatural
as if it were "upstairs," and he is needlessly put off the
Christian faith when that faith is presented in terms of,
and sometimes even said to be in some sense dependent
upon, an acceptance of the crudest conception of arbitrary divine intervention into the habitual modes of
nature's operation.

6

By this time, probably some of my readers will be
prepared to dismiss me as an "old-fashioned liberal,"
attempting to turn back the clock to nineteenth century "reduced Christianity," or even unaware of the
latest movements in the world of theology. I have no
interest in "reduced Christianity," if that means a denial
of the central assertions of Incarnation, Atonement, and
the other basic elements in historical Christianity; and
I assure my readers that I am not ignorant of recent
theological movements. In fact, I welcome much that

these movements have to teach us. But I am un-ashamed of being, in at least one sense, a "liberal." For if by that word we mean one who would wish to dwell upon the need for unity of life, experience, thought, and religion; who would welcome the truth concerning any and all of these, from whatever place that truth may come; then it seems to me that liberalism is not only a good thing, which we are in grave danger of losing today in the rush to authoritarian and totalitarian ideas, but also a profoundly and essentially Christian thing. For it depends upon faith in a God who is Lord of His whole creation and not merely sovereign in the realm of religion.

Furthermore, liberalism has been entirely right, as I see it, in its demand that Christian theology be open to continual re-statement. If this is not done, we may say with Erasmus that the result will be that orthodoxy will soon be equated with ignorance. New occasions not only "teach new duties"; they also bring to light new truths. And if all truth is from God, insofar as it is true, then we are commanded to state the Christian Gospel in such a way that it both makes room for and takes account of that which God has deigned, even in our day, to reveal to His human children—perhaps through very secular channels, indeed. And in the proc-ess of stating the Christian message in this fashion, we may discover that certain elements in the traditional presentation are peripheral to the main emphases. We may even discover that they are simply not true. For a long time, for example, it was thought that Christianity would go out the window if biblical criticism were let in at the door. We now see that this was indeed an absurd fear; a literally infallible Bible is not required by the Christian position, it is even a positive menace to the truth of the Christian view of God, man, and their relationship. Or again, it was at one time believed that if some of the Old Testament wonder-stories were denied, either in the interests of scientific veracity or in the light of biblical development, the basis of the Judaeo-Christian faith would be seriously damaged. But nowadays we believe that it is sheer gain that we are not obliged to take as history at least some of these tales.

In other words, we have learned in one area of our religion to distinguish between primary and secondary, essential and peripheral; we may perhaps be obliged to go on to say that some of those secondary or peripheral ideas can no longer be retained at all by one who in sheer honesty attempts to grasp the central and distinctive affirmations of the Christian faith.

7

But lest I now be denounced as a "dangerous modernist," appearing in the sheep's clothing of a Catholic believer, let me conclude by saying that the only variety of modernism that seems to me possible is the sort which seeks not to destroy but to construct. It may be that, in order to construct well, we must engage in some preliminary razing of unsure foundations. But our real task is to build, and to build a structure of faith which is strong enough to weather the storms of modern life and contemporary attack from the unbelieving and contemptuous. A former dean of the General Seminary once got himself in very hot water by remarking that it was often necessary to destroy the religion with which students came to study for the ministry. By this he meant that the notions about Christianity which they had imbibed elsewhere were frequently so inadequate, so open to attack, so feeble, that they would not stand up when the men got out into the active ministry. And his further insistence that a seminary's task was to replace these inadequate and inept notions by a firmly based Christian understanding should have made his meaning clear.

It is in this sense that I shall hope to speak. I for one am not at all at ease in Zion. I believe that the Christian faith faces a present and continued hostility. And I believe that it is only by the most thoroughgoing self-criticism, coupled with the most rigorous examination of our grounds for belief and our ways of believing, as well as by a careful and painstaking analysis of the Christian position itself, that we shall be able to develop a kind of Christian thought which will be storm-worthy and strong. In the kind of conflict that confronts the Christian Church, we cannot afford to be weighed down with impedimenta that are of little or no value; we must concern ourselves with the things that really matter. And we must seek to say those things in the most clear, compelling, persuasive, and (in the right sense of the word) acceptable fashion possible. This must not mean—and I have already tried to make the point and shall return to it in a later chapter—that we are to water down the Christian religion so that it becomes just another name for good will. Christianity always has and always must have about it the quality of "offense." But by this we should signify the Christian judgment upon man's sinfulness, lust, and pride, rather than its refusal to make any terms whatever with what he honestly believes to be true and what is in fact demonstrably true, unless we have been led astray by God Himself.

Or to put it in another way, it is never easy to be a Christian; but there is no sense whatsoever, so far as I can see, in making it harder than is absolutely necessary; and especially there is no sense in making it harder in an intellectual way than it must inevitably be. In my own opinion, Anglicanism is in an especially fortunate position here, for in our tradition there has been some kind of balance between the traditional and historical, the empirical and practical, and the rational or reasonable. But it is not only in Anglicanism that this kind of synthesis is to be found, although we may perhaps be pardoned for thinking that it has been peculiarly characteristic of our own tradition to hold these three in close relationship. Historical Christianity in its great sweep has been enabled to do the same thing.

My old teacher, Frank Gavin, used to say that in the Middle Ages, Dun Scotus represented the appeal to the authority of the Church with its emphasis on revelation, Bonaventura represented the appeal to religious experience and devotion, and Thomas Aquinas represented the appeal to reason and rational coherence. What we need today and shall always need is some similar inclusive unity within the Church's life. Some of us are mainly concerned to speak for the "revealed" side of our religion, while others would emphasize the experiential aspect and still a third group—with which at the moment I should wish to identify myself—would wish to maintain the reasonableness of the Christian faith in the light of all that men know and think, both yesterday and today. That is to say, the Christian Church must preach a gospel that is grounded in history and even more surely grounded in the action of God in history, which is able to validate itself in the living experience of men and women, and which is able also to vindicate itself to the enlightened and instructed reason of man. Such a gospel need not fear that it will be lacking in appeal, nor need we doubt that the victory will belong to those who preach it.

We now turn to a summary of the message which has been committed to us as Christians, for in any consideration of the problems that we have outlined in this chapter we need, first of all, to know what it is that Christianity really asserts about God, about men, about their relationship, and about the world in which that meeting takes place.

III

THE MESSAGE WE PROCLAIM

THE message which has been committed to the Christian Church is the Gospel or Good News of God who was in Christ reconciling the world to Himself. In the word which has become popular during the past few years, it is the *kerygma,* the "apostolic preaching," about Jesus the Messiah, who is Son of God. Or, in a sentence, the Christian message is Jesus Christ, and Reality interpreted through Him.

The Gospel finds its primary locus in a series of historical happenings. Of these, Holy Scripture is the record—a record that is given us in terms of the response made by a community, a people, whose reception of the revelation of God and whose rich experience is reported to us through historical material, through legend, through poetry, through prophetic utterance, through "words of wisdom," and in many other ways. The saga begins with the awakening in the Jewish mind of the conviction that, in some sense, they had been "chosen" to bring the message of the God of power, who was also the God of righteousness, to the nations of the earth. It continues with the growing awareness of the nature of this God, the demands which He makes upon men in terms of moral life, and the necessity that His holy will be proclaimed in word and deed to all peoples. An expectation that God's providential guidance of this "chosen" nation would be crowned by a special action in which He would in a unique sense "visit and redeem his people" and thus make them "a light to lighten the Gentiles," was fulfilled in the life of Jesus Christ—His birth, His teaching, His works of mercy, His death, His rising again. And in consequence of that fulfilment, the "new Israel after the Spirit" was born from the womb of the "old Israel after the flesh," and the message of life in Christ was proclaimed to the entire world.

Christianity is not the simple teaching of Jesus; it is not the imitation of His earthly life; it is not a "spiritual philosophy" built upon truths associated with His name. It is the religion which finds God in and through Jesus Christ, in consequence of which a new power is released into the hearts of men as they are united in loyalty and commitment, and in love and service, to Him "who has brought them out of darkness into his own marvellous light." It is not the "religion *of* Jesus"; it is much more the "religion *about* Jesus"; but it is above all, the religion which finds God in Jesus, as the center of a whole series of experiences which He both crowns and corrects.

Originally proclaimed in a variety of ways—"God was in Christ reconciling the world unto himself," "the Word was made flesh and dwelt among us," "while we were yet sinners, Christ died for us," "God so loved the world that he gave his only-begotten [unique] Son," and many others—it came in the course of time, and through the devout contemplation of learned men, to be seen as involving a theology or set of beliefs about God, about man, about their relationship both actual and intended, about the world, and about destiny. But the right order of things is always the preaching of Jesus and *then* the development of beliefs about Him and the implications of His life for the rest of our experience. Theology is necessary; yet it is always the result of a living faith, and a theology that is not informed by such faith is a sterile and unchristian thing.

1

Now it is inevitable that when we speak of historical events and their significance, we shall speak in the language of poetry. By this I do not mean the language of illusion, as so many Americans (whose education has all too often made them unable to grasp the reality of poetry and has turned them into prosy literalists) seem to think. Rather, I mean that in "truth embodied in a tale" we are obliged to see an element of myth and can only talk in language that is of the nature of symbol. Indeed, all significant experience must be told in that sort of speech, for the "aesthetic" aspect of experience (in Professor Whitehead's phrase) breaks through literal and scientific terminology and can only be expressed in dramatic phrase. Thus G. K. Chesterton once admonished his readers, "Don't believe in anything that can't be told in painted pictures." And whatever may be the case in regard to general human experience, it is surely the fact that all highly significant moments in life are pictorially known and understood, while history itself is much more an art than a science.

All of which is by way of saying that the report of the life of Jesus, and above all of the high moments in that life (like His birth, His "mighty works," His resurrection and ascension), is given to us not in the way in which we might read the minutes of a meeting, but through the mythopoeic (the "story-making") faculties of men who by their contact with Jesus had become not only His disciples but also His lovers and His worshippers. This will have enormous significance for the way in which we understand the element of wonder in the Gospel narratives, as we shall see when we come to discuss the problem of the miraculous in a later chapter.

2

We are now ready to set forth the message that we are to preach and teach. It will be convenient to do this under five heads: God, Christ, the Church, Man, Destiny; it is inevitable, however, that a certain overlapping will occur, because the Christian message is not a series of separated affirmations but an organic whole, finding its center and point in the Lord Jesus Christ. We cannot talk of God without thinking of His revelation in Christ, nor can we discuss the nature of Christ without considering the nature of man. This is why the Christian message can be rightly apprehended only when we take it *as a whole,* not piecemeal; it is also why the Gospel demands the surrender of the whole man, not just his intellectual assent or his emotional approval.

GOD The specifically Christian understanding of God is based, in the first instance, upon the Jewish apprehension of Him as the living God, active in history, able to reveal Himself to men in a decisive fashion, and working out through the world a purpose which will be crowned with victory. Jesus Christ does not negate this Jewish apprehension; He brings it to its fulfilment and shows the depths of meaning which are in it. Nothing is so absurd as to attempt to cut the distinctively Christian view of life from its grounding in the long tradition of Hebrew religion. However difficult we may find the interpretation of parts of the Old Testament in the light of our fuller knowledge of God's "nature and name" as Love, we cannot have a correct Christian picture of Reality unless we take into account the dynamic, holy, righteous God of the Jews. Marcionism, the ancient heresy which refused to identify the God of the Old Testament with the God of salvation in Christ, is not only a heresy but strictly nonsense, precisely because it makes nonsense out of the religious experience and interpretation of life that it attempts to state.

God, then, is conceived in the Judaeo-Christian tradition as a dynamic Being, alive with a fullness that surpasses anything known in creation. He is the supreme Reality, never to be identified with the world process, yet related to and present in that world process at every point; the creation is dependent upon Him in a fashion in which He is not Himself dependent upon it. In the language of philosophical theology, He is transcendent, more than the world; in Himself, as transcendent, He is utterly beyond our grasp. Yet He is transcendent only in such a sense that He can also be seen as immanent, or present in and at work through the world, not by some kind of remote control of events but by the immediate operation of His will and the actual reality of His presence in all things.

Christianity is not committed to any particular philosophy for the maintenance of this double truth. But it is opposed to two sets of ideas that have often found philosophical expression. It can have no sympathy with deism, the view that God at some time in the distant past set the world in operation and is now remote from it, intervening in it (if at all) only by intrusive entrances from outside in the fashion of a *deus ex machina*. The truth enshrined in deism is that Reality is not simply to be identified with the world but is more than, and other than, the world; but that truth is so exaggerated in deistic thought that God becomes an alien in His own creation. Neither can Christianity have sympathy with pantheism, which asserts precisely the opposite view to deism. In pantheism, God is not only *at one* with His world but is also *one with* it: we have here a case of *deus sive natura*. God is simply another name for the totality of the world process. The truth enshrined in pantheism is that God is nowhere absent from His creation; He informs it and moves in it and through it; His presence and power are the innermost Reality of all the proximate realities that we experience. But that truth is so exaggerated that in strictly pantheistic thought either there is no God at all, excepting in name, for everything is equally divine, or there is no world at all, since everything natural is subsumed under the term God.

The Christian view of God is theistic. It has been succinctly expressed in the medieval rhyme:

> *Extra cuncta nec exclusus*
> *Intra cuncta nec inclusus*

God is beyond all and yet not excluded from anything; He is within all, yet not included within everything. Or, in a term suggested by Baron von Hügel, the Christian view is "panentheistic"—God is more than, yet in all creation.

Furthermore, He is a God who makes Himself known.

While it is true that in His transcendent majesty He is *deus absconditus,* hidden from men, it is equally true that He wills to let men know about Him, and what is much more than that, know *Him.* By this I mean that He does not only reveal truths about Himself; He reveals Himself, and it is from His manifestation of Himself that we learn the truths about His character and His purpose. I think there can be no doubt that this Jewish element in the Christian religion is of the first importance. But it is also important to note that in revealing Himself, God is not understood to be quite so selective as some modern theologians would suggest. There is indeed a particular revelation to the Jews; and later, as Christians believe, there is a special revelation in Jesus Christ. But there is also a general revelation: God wills to let Himself be known—or more adequately stated, God wills to make Himself known—in other places than in Palestine and to other people than the "chosen race." As Jewish religious thought developed, this notion of a diffused self-revelation of God became more and more explicit and reached a climax in the great prophet whom we call the Second Isaiah. Anything that may be said about the particularity of the divine self-disclosure to the Jews must be set against the background of a universal self-disclosure to all men as they are prepared by God to learn, in divers portions and through various avenues, something of His wisdom, power, and purpose.

Again, God is a Being who in His revelation of Himself is shown to be "personal" in nature. By this the Christian has never meant that God is simply man writ large, with the limitations inherent in human individuality. Rather He has meant that God is so related to men that they must think of Him as at least possessed of that integration in His nature, that capacity to respond to and communicate with His creation, that wisdom in acting and freedom to act, which can best be described by thinking of Him more after the analogy of personality than impersonality—God may be and must be called "He" rather than "it." Because He is in this sense personal, He may rightly be understood to have a purpose and to work for the effecting of that purpose. As the controller of nature and history, He is able to use both of them in their dependence upon Him; and through them and in them to accomplish ends which He has set before Him.

Finally, these ends and purposes are good; hence it is declared that the God who wills and effects them is also good, although His goodness may be beyond our understanding. The problem of evil in the world is met by the Christian faith not with a denial of its reality but with a triumphant affirmation that God is able to conquer evil and that man is called upon to have his share in the extermination of evil from the world. So far as I know, there has never been an "official" Christian explanation of why evil is in the world; but there has always been a consistently Christian way of handling evil, and that is through faith in God and by the power of Jesus Christ.

43

CHRIST For historical Christianity, Jesus Christ is no mere prophet or teacher or sage. He is the peculiarly direct action of God in human history. On the other hand, He is genuinely human in the whole range of His life and experience as a man. This double judgment has been expressed historically in the dogma of the Incarnation, in which it is asserted that Jesus Christ is truly divine, truly human, and truly the personal union of the two.

The conviction that this is the case does not arise out of idle specualtion or the perhaps inevitable human desire to exalt a great hero of the race. It arises from a participation in that which theology has called the "benefits" of Christ; that is, from a knowledge of and sharing in the results of His total life, death, and resurrection. He has brought to men newness of life, given them hope and courage, released them from the bondage of sin, opened to them new possibilities of victory over evil both in themselves and in the world. And since it would appear that no man could accomplish these things, Christian faith has dared to assert that this Man is more than a man; He is also, in a real sense, so related to God that it may be said of Him that God lived and worked in Him as in no other. Even more, it has dared to declare, the way in which God lived and worked in Him was of such an intimate and direct nature that His humanity is the instrument for Deity, His total human life the life of God translated into human terms.

Since God has so lived and worked amongst us in the

humanity of Jesus Christ, we have new knowledge of God's character. Not only is He good; He is also a God of love. "God so loved the world that he gave his only-begotten Son . . ." Because He gave His Son, we know He loves His human children; because He loves His human children, we know He loves His whole creation. "His nature and his name is love." But the love which is of God, and which in one sense *is* God, is not sentimentality; it is the austere and exacting love which could use the Cross to accomplish its ends and which could demand of the beloved the utter commitment of life. This is not cheap love; it is terrible love, judging men in their shallowness and rousing them to heights which mere sentimentality could never envisage, much less establish for men.

In the light of this historical fact of the coming of Jesus Christ, but also in the light of the equally certain historical fact that His coming was met by a response so swift, so compelling, and so profound, the Christian Church has gone on to make a further statement about God Himself. That statement is that God is no bare unity, but that in the mystery of the divine life there is a richness of relationships bearing some resemblance to our own human social belonging. God is the Creative Source, the Father; He is the Expressive Act, the Son; He is the Responsive Movement, the Spirit who drives men to conform to His will and opens their lives to His presence. He is, then, Trinity-in-Unity and Unity-in-Trinity, not only in His operation in the creation but also, in a mystery beyond our finite human comprehension, in the depths of His own inner life. And this affirmation means something else: it means that all the revealing, redeeming, healing influences and operations in history are the work of that same Expressive Act of God, the Word, who was focally and decisively en-manned in Jesus; and it means that all the responding movements to such influences and operations are the work of the same Spirit, who is known in Christian experience as the Holy Spirit given through Christ.

THE CHURCH The coming of Jesus Christ into the world at a given time and place is extended in history through a community that is so intimately linked with His life and so effectively the instrument of His power that it can be called His Body. This is the Holy Church, composed in actual fact of all men who have been caught up into response to Jesus Christ, and composed potentially of all men, everywhere and at all times, who have in them the stuff that makes possible that response. Of the structures and sacramental life of the Church we cannot speak here; it must suffice to say that historical Christianity has never been content to regard the Church as an amorphous entity but has always seen it as a positive observable reality which, in its human imperfection and sin, is none the less *in the divine intention* the spotless Bride of Christ, whose means of grace are our surest way to a saved and saving life and whose mission in the world is to bring men of every race and nation and class into the God-man relationship established in Jesus Christ.

MAN   For the Christian Church, man is the creature of God, made in His image, yet fallen into sin. But beyond that, man is also the sinful creature who may be redeemed from sin into newness of life. Hence a defeatist attitude about human nature is an impossibility, while at the same time a facile perfectionism is seen to be absurd. I do not think it is necessary for me to develop this particular theme at any length, since the main task of most of our modern theologians has been to discuss the Christian view of man, and their teaching is familiar to most of us. It is important to note, however, that Christians see man not simply as a person, but as *a person in community,* and they can never be content, if they know their religion, with the sort of individualism which would pretend that a man can live to, work for, and find happiness in, himself alone.

It is also important to note that Christianity has thought of man not as a soul imprisoned in a body, from which one day he will be freed. On the contrary, it has thought of him as a total personality, mind-body-and-relationships; and whatever it may have to say about human destiny can only be understood if this kind of unity of personality is first rightly apprehended.

DESTINY   Christianity cannot regard man's mortal existence in this world of space and time, as

47

all there is to him. Man is made for a destiny which this world is neither big enough to contain nor adequate to express. God has, in fact, so created man that he may move towards more complete integration of his personality in God and His will; death, for such an one, means the end of this mortal existence but, through it and beyond it, God, who first created human personality, can and will re-create it so that in the integrity of his increasingly God-centered personality man with his fellows may find fulfilment. On the other hand, God has created man with sufficient freedom—which is part of what is meant when we speak of man's being in God's image—to choose, not integration in God but wilful isolation from God; and the end of that choice, if persisted in and left without opening to the healing influence of the divine mercy, is self-alienation from God, which is hell. The Christian Church has never said who, if any, have persisted in such self-alienation; it has only recognized, with a complete realism, that human freedom makes such alienation possible and that the denial of the possibility is at the same time the denial of human freedom and moral responsibility.

Finally, the Christian message affirms that "in the end," wherever and whenever and however that may be, God will accomplish His purpose in the whole process of creation; and although we can only speak of these things in symbols and "as in a glass darkly," it has declared that when the "end" comes, God will be "all in all." He will have "accomplished the number of His elect," sat in "final judgment," and brought to pass the "new creation" in which all things shall be fair.

3

Now I realize that in this brief sketch I have hardly said all that should be said, while I also realize that in a way I have said much more than should be said. But I have sought to state the Gospel and its implications as these have been thought out by the great central stream of Christian experience. And I have tried to put that Gospel and its implications in as simple, yet adequate, a fashion as I could.

But it is obvious that even when stated in such a way, the whole problem of semantics at once arises. Despite the effort to avoid them, I have been compelled to use words which mean little to modern men, and I could have used a great many others that would be equally without meaning. In this connection, I may be permitted to recall an experience of my own, many years ago. I was invited to an evening meeting with some friends who were entertaining a discussion club in a small suburban community. The particular topic for the evening was religion; and my friends asked me not to let it be known that I was a clergyman, for they thought that such knowledge might inhibit the members of the club from free discussion of the theme. After a long and, in many ways, illuminating evening, each member of the group including myself was asked to make some comments. I did so; and it was fairly obvious that I was a Christian.

At this point, one of the company turned to me and asked: "Do you believe that 'there's a fountain filled with blood, drawn from Emmanuel's veins'?" I sensed something of his difficulty, so I answered: "Yes and no. No, if you mean that I should myself find the words that you have quoted particularly apt if I had to state my own beliefs apart from traditional language. Yes, if you mean that I accept the real significance which those words, unfortunate as they may be, are trying to express." My questioner immediately responded: "Well, what is it that they are trying to express?" And I answered, not very adequately but as well as I could on a moment's notice: "These words and formulae are attempting to describe certain facts of human experience. When men and women really come to understand themselves and their human situation, they begin to recognize their impotence to meet life's demands and to solve its problems. And when they courageously face this fact, they know that they stand in need of a source of power and of deliverance from guilt. They further know that, because of something that happened in history a long time ago, experience of this source of power and of this deliverance from guilt is possible; and they know this is an immediately available reality if they will now respond to it. By virtue of this response, and by virtue of it alone, human life is once again invested with dignity."

That was a long-winded reply to a simple question. But I wonder if I could have done anything else in that situation? Certainly the man who asked me the question would not have understood or accepted the language of theology; and I gravely doubt if talk about sin, original and actual, atonement by Christ, justification, and sanctification would have made much sense to him. As it was, he said, "I should like to believe that." I do not know what happened afterward, but I have always felt that perhaps I was "guided," at that moment, to say something that opened for him the door to Christian discipleship.

You will realize that I tell this story with no egotistic motive, but simply because the incident made perfectly plain to me that the semantic problem is one of our chief difficulties today with large groups of people. And I fancy that any Christian minister who is honest with himself will confess that, to a considerable degree, his failure to make the Christian message come alive has been due to his inability to talk in a language that can be "understanded of the people."

4

There is no easy solution of this problem. But you will let me make several suggestions which may help towards a solution. First, it is imperative that we think through for ourselves what the Christian message really means. Far too often we have been content to accept it, without ever really appropriating it for ourselves. I do not wish to suggest that we are dishonest; I mean simply that because the ancient and hallowed words have a profound value for us, we have been ready to repeat them, without realizing the importance of such rephrasing as shall vitalize them for ourselves and make them vital for others.

For this reason, I can think of no better exercise for a minister than to set down on paper, with the use of none of the traditional language, exactly what this or that element in the Christian faith really means for him. I have often urged this discipline upon my theological students as the best way known to me for a parish priest to secure fresh insight into the great heritage which is his. And not long ago I myself attempted to do this for the whole of the Nicene Creed, in an attempt to make this contemporary for myself. I put this rewriting here, not to suggest that it is entirely correct and flawless, but as an example of the sort of thing I have in mind:

We place our whole trust and confidence for time and for eternity in One Eternal Divine Reality, Creative Source of all things material and spiritual, caring in a fatherly fashion for His whole creation and for us His human creatures.

And in One Eternal Self-Expression of Divine Reality, called the Word or Son, who is of the same stuff as Reality Himself, not a created being but an eternally subsisting mode of the Divine Life. He, being that Self-Expression of Reality through whose agency all things were created and are even now sustained in being, manifested and operative throughout the creation and chiefly in our regard

52

as ground of human personality, for us men and for our wholeness of life, expressed Himself focally and decisively in a true and complete human life, of body, mind, and spirit, born of Mary. In that human life which was lived amongst us—sharing our lot, suffering, condemned to the Cross under Pontius Pilate, dying as all men die—He was victorious over death and took back to God the human life in which He had conquered evil, sin, and the power of death itself; in that life He reigns over men and through Him we have new access to the Divine Reality; He judges and shall judge both living and dead, for His is an endless rule over created things.

And we trust in the Spirit who is God's Responsive Action through His creation, Himself truly Divine, who gives life to men as in Him they respond to God's Self-Expression, signally in their response to Jesus Christ as focal Self-Expression in human terms; who also gives life to all else, as in varying degree it responds to God's Self-Expression wherever it may be; who is one with God the Creative Source and God's Self-Expression in the One Divine Life and with both is adored and given glory; who was ever at work before, and is still at work apart from, the focal Self-Expression in Jesus Christ.

And we trust one society, divinely given and organically one, whose life and message are continuous with earliest Christian days and have been given men through the impact of Jesus Christ's life, death, and

53

victory. We acknowledge one baptism by virtue of which we are made members of that society and given the possibility of new life with Divine Reality. And we look with confidence and expectation to our share in Christ's victory and participation in eternal life with Divine Reality through Him, an eternal life which death can never destroy.

Every major assertion of the eucharistic creed is, I believe, included in this rewriting. And so far as possible all traditional language has been extruded. The rewriting is obviously not intended as a substitute for the ancient hymn of faith; it is a strictly personal exercise intended for the study and not for the sanctuary or pulpit. But once the job is done, it is amazing how much more vivid the great affirmations become to oneself and how much more compellingly one can proclaim them and teach them in idiom that our contemporaries can understand.

Further, we need to know, not by rote, but by heart. We need to know "on our pulses," as John Keats put it. We need to apprehend, as clearly as possible and as simply as possible, the things that are beyond question the master-light of our seeing. Above all, we need to discriminate what one might call the minimal Christian assertions—without which Christianity would not be Christianity at all, but something else. Here once again, a simple exercise will be of great help. I think that the surest way of accomplishing these ends is by putting down in as brief and terse a fashion as possible the affirmations which a Christian must make if he is to retain the reality of the Christian interpretation of life and experience within the fellowship of the Christian community.

Some time ago I did this for myself, using as the basis for my little *credo* a suggested revision of the ancient creeds made a quarter of a century ago by Professor Bethune-Baker. Here is the result:

I believe in God our Father, maker and sovereign-ruler of all things. And in Jesus Christ His Son our Lord, incarnate Word of God, in whom very God dwelt in very man; who lived among us a true human life, was crucified for us, rose from the dead, and is alive for evermore. And in the Spirit of the Father and the Son, worshipped together with Them in the unity of Godhead; one holy Catholic Church; one baptism into Christ for the forgiveness of sins; one Eucharist; one fellowship of the faithful in heaven and in earth. And in the life of the world to come, in God's victory over sin, evil, and death, and in His kingdom which shall have no end.

In this quite personal *credo* I sought to put the things which a Christian could not possibly refuse without at the same time relinquishing his right to be called a Christian in any historically recognizable sense of the word. The omissions are as significant as the inclusions; for it is my conviction that much which is historically interesting and valuable is not of the "heart of the matter";

and that while we should never seek to whittle down the big assertions, we must maintain an indifference to much which may or may not be true, having confidence that the Spirit, who guides the Church, will lead us into ever fuller and better understanding of the things that belong to our peace. There is much that is peripheral and secondary in the heritage which is ours; this we are not to deny, excepting when such denial is imposed upon us by loyalty to the Spirit of truth, but we are certainly not to insist upon it as if it were what really mattered in the Christian interpretation of life. Our great historical creeds come to us from the rich tradition of which we are part; we say them joyfully because they are symbols of our Christian continuity and our unity in faith with those who have gone before us. They are pointers on our way, not stop signs forbidding further thought and exploration. When interpreted in this fashion, they are no longer the obstacles that they often seem to be to those who think that, if they repeat them at all, they must repeat them in the most literal sense. It is a sorry thing when the credal affirmations are treated as if they were hurdles to be jumped, one after another, by those who would run the Christian race.

5

Secondly, I believe that we need to be much more alert than we usually are to the actual idiom of our time. It is not necessary that we should read every new book or listen to every new song; we do not have any obligation to reek of contemporaneity. But it is necessary that we should listen to what people are saying, catch the particular accent of their speech, and seek to think with them as they talk quite popularly and unself-consciously about non-religious matters. The professional and technical jargon of the theological classroom and the dogmatics textbook has its own importance. It is a convenient kind of shorthand for those of us who are engaged in this enterprise. Furthermore, the knowledge and use of such language, in appropriate circles, is our only certain way of linking our Christian thought with that of the tradition whose spearhead we are. But just as shorthand means little to those who have not thoroughly studied and properly mastered it, so our common theological talk means little or nothing to those who are outside the Christian Church and often to those who are within it. We need to learn to talk in the language of these people, rather than to try to make them talk in ours.

One of the best sermons that I have ever heard was delivered by a distinguished and deeply orthodox preacher. But what he said about the meaning of life in grace was said so simply, so easily, so understandably that any member of the congregation could grasp it and relate it all to his own experience. Nor was there any suggestion that, at bottom, this was really a superficially easy matter; instead, the preacher made us see, by the illustrations he employed and the relation of his words to the common human experience of mystery beyond our explaining, that a whole lifetime would not exhaust the implications of the simple truth that a Christian's life is lived in the grace of our Lord Jesus Christ. Is it any wonder that the parish which that preacher serves is wonderfully alive, with a congregation who know Him in whom they have believed and who recognize that to be a Christian is the highest of all adventures?

6

Finally, I am sure that we can accomplish little unless we learn to speak to people exactly where they live. We must "speak to their condition," not to some imagined situation in which we should like to find them. If, for example, the concept of sin is to come alive for our contemporaries, we must not talk to them of sin as a specifically religious concept and then be irritated or distressed because they do not seem to know what we are talking about. Sin, in that profound sense, is only recognized for what it is when men have entered deeply enough into the reality of the God-man relationship to know the horror of man's alienation from God and his estrangement from the ultimate ground of his being. But the average man's sense of failure, his feeling of frustration, his knowledge that he lets other people down, his awareness of the radical imperfection of even the best that he tries to do, his awful loneliness and his recognition of estrangement from others through self-assertiveness and pretension, are real and vivid enough for anyone to see. It is precisely in the "secular" areas—in one sense of that word; for in another there are no such areas at all, since God is the ground of being and the Reality in all realities, however "secular"—that men do sin; when this is understood we can then move on to the specifically "religious" concept of sin as disobedience to the will of God and the disruption of man's rightful relationship to Him.

It is one of the great services rendered to the modern world by non-Christians like Lionel Trilling and Arthur Schlesinger, Jr., that in their discussions of literature and politics they have been able to translate the notion of sin into terms meaningful for modern readers. But it is a tragedy that we Christian preachers and teachers did not do it long ago. I suppose that among living American Christian thinkers, Reinhold Niebuhr is one of the few who have accomplished just this; and I suspect that the explanation of the extraordinary influence of Dr. Niebuhr is, to a large degree, found in the fact that when he talks of sin, men know that he is talking to them where they are, and as they are, and so he makes sense.

What I have said about the concept of sin might equally well have been said about other Christian assertions, other elements in our message. To take one more illustration, have we recognized sufficiently the value of the non-religious names of God? One recalls that St. Augustine was ready to describe, and even to address, God in his *Confessions* by names which were not at all specifically religious. "Beauty ever old yet ever knew," "Truth," "Goodness," "Excellence": here are some names

59

which he used and which he evidently found valuable. If we can bring men to see something of the meaning of God by talking of Him, as I am wont to do, as "Reality *itself*," we may then be able to go on and talk about Him as "Reality *Himself*," Reality who speaks to men and works in them to bring them to Himself; and thus proceed to talk about the nature and purpose, as well as the demands and succour, that Reality, God, may imply for men.

Rudolf Bultmann has said that in an age when we light our houses by electricity, it does not make much sense to talk of demon-possession. We may add that it *does* make sense to talk of neuroses and psychoses, because they are part of a total unity of life and experience which men and women know and understand. But that points us beyond the problem of semantics, of words and phrases and their meaning, to the even deeper problem of forms of thought. It is with that problem that we shall be concerned in the two following chapters.

IV

THE DIVINE REALITY
AND THE CREATED WORLD

I have said that the "forms of thought"—that is to say, the set of mind or way of approach to the understanding of one's world—which are familiar to our contemporaries have little relationship to much which appears to be said in the Christian tradition. The controversy which has raged, since the war, in the German Church is concerned with this problem. The distinguished New Testament scholar, Rudolf Bultmann, published an essay in which he urged the need for what he called "de-mythologizing" the Christian message. In fact what he was urging was "re-mythologizing" it, for he argued that it is only in the terms of the existentialist world-view (particularly as that has been stated in the writings of Heidegger) that the Gospel can have significance for modern man. Such a world view, like all philosophical visions, is mythological in nature; it could not be otherwise since man cannot have a literal and precise knowledge of the sum of things entire.

Bultmann's original essay, with the many answers to it, has been published in a volume edited by H. W. Bartsch, along with a response to his critics by Bultmann himself. Parts of the large German work have appeared in English, and already some discussion of the question has taken place in our own country as well as in Britain. As a writer in an English journal (J. S. Bezzant, in *Theology* for June, 1954) has noted, the real importance of the controversy, whether in its German form or in the English-speaking world, is not so much in the solutions that Bultmann proposes to his own queries, as it is in the proof which it offers that the difficulties which an older liberalism and various kinds of continental and English modernism were concerned to meet are by no means dead. The revivals of neo-orthodoxy and of confessional theology on the continent of Europe and in America, and the renascent Catholic orthodoxy in Anglican circles, as well as the so-called "biblical theology" which has followed the long period of intensive critical study of Scripture, have succeeded only in shelving for a time a set of difficulties which once again are making themselves strongly felt.

And those difficulties are the sort which may be

summed up in the phrase that I have used: forms of thought. It is not merely a question of "relevance," of making points of contact between actual human situations and the gospel of salvation. It is even more seriously a question of a total view of the world which, through the influence of modern scientific study and its findings, and through the diffused influence of a new metaphysical approach that is largely the result of scientific research and its presuppositions, has become much more widespread than we often like to think. This cannot be countered by talking of "scientolatry," as does a recent writer, for it is not a matter of men's worshipping science and its way of seeing the world. Rather it is the problem of incorporating into Christian thought a general view of existence which is no mere guesswork but, so far as any human discovery can be, a true picture of things as they are.

I realize that to talk in this way is likely to earn the contempt of that school of religious writers who sneer at modern science, thumb their noses at recent philosophies like Whitehead's, and assert that Christianity not only has nothing to fear from, but also nothing to learn from, any of the work of contemporary scientists and philosophers. For reasons stated in earlier chapters I reject entirely and completely this superior attitude towards those who have in fact changed modern man's whole way of seeing life and the world in which he lives. And it is in the conviction that Christianity has much to learn from these modern students and thinkers, and that it can only be presented understandably if it takes full account of their work, that I am writing this book.

1

The first question that suggests itself has to do with the symbolic nature of our theological language. The words of our liturgies seem to imply, although they do not necessarily demand, a kind of "deistic" view of God in relation to His creation. We speak much of God's "visiting" His people, as if He came to them from outside their world; we talk of Him as if He were "above" in a spatial sense, so that when He comes to us He must come "down." Even the word "come" might carry the implication that He is not here but must move from some other "place" to the place where we are. Indeed, the phrases both of popular and of official devotion might be thought to describe a universe which is remote from its Creator; a universe into which, on particular occasions and in special ways, He intrudes Himself in order to accomplish certain ends or answer certain prayers.

Now there can be no doubt that symbolically such language is often apt. Furthermore, it is difficult, if not impossible, to think of any other way in which we humans can talk save by the use of terms drawn from spatial and temporal experience such as ours must necessarily be. Edwyn Bevan, in his important book, *Belief and Symbol,* has rightly emphasized that many of the symbolic phrases which we use have a certain natural quality about them —it is, for instance, a natural use of words to speak of heaven as "above," since the spatial idea of that which is superior to man is naturally related to that which, in the order of significance and the order of being, is superior to him. I believe that Bevan is right. It would be absurd to attempt to change the language of liturgy and the language of private devotion so that it would be entirely accurate in terms of a modern cosmology and our new understanding of the way in which God must be seen as related to His world. We are still quite content to speak of "the sun rising in the morning" and "setting in the evening," although we are well aware of the inaccuracy of this mode of predication. And we readily talk of "the shaking of Wall Street" when what we really mean is that the stocks and bonds bought and sold there have, as we say in still another kind of symbolic phrase, "taken a tumble."

But as another, and perhaps more profound, writer on these matters has insisted, we dare not forget that our words *are* symbols, and we must be careful lest we treat them as if they had a precise and literal denotation. I am referring to Professor Wilbur Marshall Urban's discussion in *Language and Reality,* a book that I believe ought to be required reading for all the clergy. Professor Urban, especially in his chapter on the language of religion and theology, has made very clear the fact that all language used of God and of God's relationship to His world, and, above all, the language employed in Christian worship and in private devotion, has the nature of symbol and, therefore, is understandable, in any really profound sense, only by those who approach it with a poetic mind.

And, despite the dangers to which his position is exposed, Alan W. Watts (whose departure from the Christian faith was a great loss to him and to us) had a point that was well worth making when, in his study *The Supreme Identity,* he carefully distinguished between the implicit metaphysic of religion and the symbolic language in which the religious and theological statements about God must be made. Mr. Watts vitiated his point, for us at least, when he implied that the metaphysic of religion is fundamentally that of Vedanta philosophy; but the point itself is important, and we are not obliged to say that the particular philosophy to which this author, on quite special grounds, feels himself attracted is the philosophy—the "frame of reference" or the "structure of meaning"—which we should wish to defend.

This distinction between modes of speech is not a particularly modern one. Plato, for instance, intimated it; it was conventional in the Neoplatonic thinkers; and in St. Thomas Aquinas the constant emphasis upon analogical predication as that mode of speech which is to be employed when discussing God and His relation to the world points towards the same necessity of symbolical, rather than literal, language about divine things. God and His world are related in such a fashion, St. Thomas saw, that we dare not presume to speak univocally— that is, with a literal and precise implication for our words; on the other hand, we must not speak equivocally, as if the words that we use (and that are drawn from our own experience) have no relationship whatsoever to the nature of divine Reality. Rather we must speak with that analogical use of words which sees that our experience points towards, but in a considerable degree is negated by, the transcendent reference which we are seeking to make.

The trouble is that it is very easy to fall into the error of mistaking language which is symbolically apt for language that is meant to be literally precise. We then teach and preach in terms of this mistaken identification, so that our hearers come to think that Christians believe in a two-storey world, with the natural order on one level and the divine order on another. They assume, from our literalistic speech, that since the two orders are discontinuous, we believe that there is a necessity for intervention in a similarly literalistic sense, with the inevitable disordering (if I may be pardoned the pun) of the lower order by the higher.

I should not wish, for a moment, to change the symbolical language of liturgy. But I believe that it is quite possible to help our people to recognize that it *is* symbolical language; and that precisely because it is symbolical, it is all the more evocative of meaning, full of "power," apt for the expression of our ideas. On the other hand, we can see that when we move from the strictly liturgical expression of our faith and seek to present it in intellectual terms that will bring it into direct relationship with the forms of thought of our contemporaries, we can use the language which is normal in that sphere and show that the Christian faith is as capable of giving meaning to such a world view as it once was of giving meaning to earlier and now rejected views of the nature of the world process.

2

Nowhere, I think, is the fallacy of literalistic interpretation of symbolic language more apparent than in the popular understanding—it would be better to say misunderstanding—of the religious significance of the concept of the miraculous.

There cannot be the slightest doubt, to my mind, that the ordinary person who hears about miracles, and I must add the supposedly instructed person who often talks about them, will be likely to conclude that God is thought to be *outside* His creation, in what is practically a spatial sense, but that He is believed to act now and again within it by some catastrophic interference with its ordering. This is taking literally the deistic implications of symbolical speech. Note that I am not saying that this is the idea of the miraculous entertained by those who stand as our greatest theologians. I have often thought that St. Augustine, who made the distinction between the kind of wonder which is *contra naturam* and the miracle which is *supra quam nota est naturae,* would be horrified by the popular defense of the notion of miracle often found in books of Christian apologetic. St. Augustine's view may not be satisfactory, but at least it did not suppose that God made intrusions into the order of nature;

rather it insisted that nature means that which is known to us of God's ways of working in ordinary and regular fashion, while events which have an unprecedented quality and awaken faith in him who beholds them or hears of them, are not *contrary to* God's ways of working but *above* that which hitherto or elsewhere we have seen of those ways of working. Likewise, St. Thomas Aquinas, whose metaphysic was to a large degree founded upon his acceptance of the varieties of causation enumerated in the Aristotelian writings, could hardly have assented to a view which suggested that God had to intrude into His world to set it right or to make Himself known. For St. Thomas God upheld the entire creation by His essence, His power, and His purpose; and the different events and experiences known in the course of the creation were assigned to different modes of the divine operation rather than to intrusive acts from outside the creation. Once again, St. Thomas's view may not be satisfactory, especially in view of the metaphysical revolution brought about during the past century and expressed by thinkers like Professor Whitehead, but at any rate it did not rest upon a non-theistic picture of the world.

The kind of defense of miracle found in Mr. C. S. Lewis's book *Miracles* is not only beside the point, in that the naturalism which he attacks is a naturalism which no modern naturalist would wish to defend. It is not only appallingly indifferent to the findings of biblical criticism, in its indiscriminate lumping of miracle stories from the Synoptic Gospels with those related in the Fouth Gospel.

Above all, it is based upon a set of metaphysical assumptions concerning the relation of God to His world which are incredible in the light of all that we now know on this matter, while its quasi-deistic picture of God (which is implied throughout, and which in other books by Mr. Lewis seems almost to delight in) is impossible of acceptance by anyone who has sought seriously to understand the real implications of the Christian world view. I am not sure that Mr. Lewis's book is dishonest; but I am very sure that it is disingenuous.

3

For the real significance of the concept of the miraculous, its historical value in religious and theological reference, is to insist that *God is not bound to His creation, on the one hand, although He is everywhere present in and at work in it; but that He is able, on the other, to act with greater intensity here than there, now than then.* The meaning of the concept is exactly that which is stated, as I think much more adequately and satisfactorily, in the Christian and Hebrew conception of the providential operation of God in His world. The God of providence is the God who is not prisoner of His creation, but in it and through it is able to work freely, yet in terms which He Himself has laid down, for the accomplishment of His purposes. It has the particular value also of introducing a "personal" note into the whole matter, since it is *God* who is seen to be at work, and we are not confused by references to levels or orders which interact or intervene one upon another.

It is for this reason that I myself am inclined to think that we might well give up the use of the word "miracle." It has gathered about it so many unhappy, unfortunate, and indeed mistaken associations, by this time impossible to remove, that it introduces confusion and doubt at precisely the point where we need assurance and faith. The conception of providence, however, carrying with it (as I have said) a much more personal implication, will serve very well for our purposes; and I am in entire agreement with James M. Thompson, who many years ago in his illuminating and now little-known book *From Fact to Faith,* sought to make this point and suffered for it at the hands of English ecclesiastical authority.

Perhaps I may quote here some remarks of Dr. William Porcher DuBose, America's only really great Anglican theologian, who wrote nearly forty years ago:

I confess that I hold the truth of a universal and particular providence more firmly and I believe more really than I ever did before. I believe in a personal providence in nature, because I believe that nature is God, is how God is and acts in those things that we call natural . . . God in natural things acts naturally and never contradicts or is inconsistent with Himself. Insofar then as His providence is in and through natural things, there is no deviation by any hair's breadth from the course of what we call the causation of nature. And yet, within the course of nature, if any Christian man will, as St. Paul says, love God and enter into the meaning and operation of His eternal and divine purpose, I know that he will find that literally all things are working together, that God is working all things together, for his individual and particular good.

That quotation, I believe, gives us the clue to the right relationship of nature and supernature, the world and God. For, as he says in the same context, the religiously significant point here is that God "never fails to help those whom He brings up in his steadfast fear and love. I cannot see where God ever promises to change natural things or natural sequences for us. I do see where He promises that in them all and through them all we shall be more than conquerors."[1]   And a rethinking of the whole idea along such lines, with due recognition of the fact that, after all, we are theists who find that "nature is how God is and acts in those things that we call natural," will deliver us from that nest of difficulties which science must inevitably introduce with its firm conviction, still unshaken and it would appear unshakable, that the "course of nature" is consistent and non-contradictory.

It is not necessary to go all the way with Professor

[1] William P. DuBose, *Turning Points in My Life* (New York: Longmans Green and Co., 1912), pp. 85-86. Used by permission of the publisher.

Charles Hartshorne in his several recent books (of which, perhaps, the most important is *The Divine Relativity*) to see that it is by a "pan-en-theistic" view of God and nature that we can most readily meet the attack of science on the religious interpretation of nature. Baron von Hügel was, so far as I know, one of the first, if not the first, to use this term; Professor Hartshorne has developed the idea in important directions. By it we mean that God and His world, supernature and nature, are not related deistically, but that at every point and at all times, there is an interpenetration of the world by God whose presence and power are both the ground of existence and the creative purpose which works through existence. And God is the kind of God He is because this is the kind of world in which He is ceaselessly active, just as much as that this world is what it is because God is what He is.

4

What has been called, then, in traditional language a miraculous event is more properly understood as a concentration or intensification or, if you will, a focussing of the universally present and generally pervasive divine activity. Such concentration is in one sense a *new* thing, since it brings to bear upon given situations an intensified divine power and makes available a particular divine presence; but in another sense it is not new, since it is *God* who is here at work and since, in His working, His purpose and achievement ever remain constant in aim and self-consistent in character. It is, indeed, the doctrine of God which is at stake here; some versions of what is called orthodoxy are really not orthodox at all, since they presuppose a God who lacks the integrity and self-consistency which the entire Judaeo-Christian tradition has made one of His most significant attributes.

What we ought to say is that there is, as it were, a pervasive and general operation of God in His creation, precisely as there is a pervasive and general presence of God in His creation. But this is not all, although this must be affirmed over and over again lest we fall into the error of the absentee deity. It must also be said that there is something else again—a concentration, an intensification, a focussing if you will, of God's presence and operation. This occurs at special times and in special places and for special ends. It does not contradict or deny the pervasive action, but crowns and completes that action. It gives us the key or clue to the meaning of the whole movement of God in and through and with His world; it corrects partial misunderstanding and opens our eyes to see new depths of reality and of grace. Nor is it merely a matter of "showing." It is above all a matter of "doing" and of "imparting." When God is thus seen as concentrated, His action intensified, His presence and power focussed, new energies are released and men are lifted to newer and more complete levels of life and experience.

This is exactly what one might expect in a world such

as we have now come to know through the devoted labours of those like Professor Whitehead and many others,
who have worked valiantly towards a metaphysic which
will be congruent with the newer physics, the newer
biology, the newer view of man as a psycho-socio-physio-
logical creature. What is even more, it is exactly what we
find when we take the biblical world view as a whole and
do not permit ourselves to be bogged down with its cosmological mythology. It is here that Professor Bultmann
is both right and wrong. He is entirely correct in seeing
that we simply cannot think any longer in terms of the
biblical *welt-bild,* or cosmological mythology, drawn from
a primitive cosmogony. He is in error when he appears
to confuse this with the biblical *weltanschauung,* the
total picture of God and man and their relationships in
a world which is God's creation and in which He is ceaselessly at work. It is one of the unfortunate results of our
present-day revival of what is called "biblical theology"
that some of its most ardent exponents appear not to
be content with showing the absolute necessity for Christianity of the great *motifs* that run through Scripture
and bind it into a remarkable unity, but fall victim to the
desire to resurrect a cosmological mythology which is
beyond the belief of any modern man. And it is even
more unfortunate that almost all the advocates of biblical
theology fail to see that while it is precisely in the symbolic language of Scripture that we must find our Christian materials for faith, this does not imply that we can-

not take this material and yet, for purposes of adequate statement in the world of today, put this poetic and symbolic understanding in a framework which is the result of careful and patient meditation on that which even in our own time God is graciously revealing, through science and many other avenues of man's quest, concerning Himself and His ways with His creation.

5

I do not wish to enter here into the further question of particular instances of what is called "miracle." It will suffice to say that such concentrations, intensifications, and focussings of God's providential action in His world, as I have described and insisted upon, are reported for us in Scripture, although it would be absurd to say that there have been no such instances in areas with which Scripture is not concerned. Furthermore, it will suffice to say that Christianity could perfectly well be conceived without miracle, in the sense of a multiplicity of special occurrences which are associated, say, with the person of Jesus Christ, but it could never be conceived or maintained without that providential ordering of history which for our faith reached its culmination in Jesus Christ. He is *the* concentration, intensification, focussing, of God's action in the world, so far as we men are concerned. This point was well made by Professor A. E. Taylor in his discussion of the subject in *The Faith of a Moralist*. I should only wish to add that the idea of the

Supernatural—*if* by this is meant not some extra storey above the created world but the divine Reality Himself as being in His metaphysical nature more than and (in symbolic language) "above" the world yet operative without fail "within it"—is, as Professor Taylor also noted, essential to the whole Christian picture. We may not like the term, because of its unhappy associations with the two-storey picture of the world; the idea itself, when rightly understood, is utterly necessary.

As to the particular reported instances of unprecedented event, then, we shall subject them to the same sort of rigorous historical examination which we give to all stories which come to us from the past. Some of them we can see as closely related to known experience, as in the case of the faith healings recounted in Scripture. Some of them we can interpret as the ways in which, to a people whose thinking was mythopoeic and whose faith in Christ was already high, the significance they found in Him could best be stated. Some of them we can see as resting upon a more primitive picture of nature than our own, or on a genuine and honest misunderstanding of some event of which early Christians heard years after it had occurred. All of them can best be understood if we recognize that they are deliverances of faith as it received and handed on traditions of the life, action, death, and victory over death, of Jesus Christ their Lord and ours. At any rate, we shall not let our own joyous acceptance of the Gospel the primitive Church preached be dependent upon a literal reading of the story they told about that One in whom they, and we, find that life and immortality have been brought to light.

6

If the argument of this chapter has any merit, we may be sure that the acceptance of the Christian faith does not demand that we give up what is sound and good in that view of the world which comes to us from scientific research and philosophical meditation on the results of that research. And this leads to a final consideration, which as it seems to me is of special importance at this time.

Under the influence of the theological revival of our day, to which all of us owe so much, there has been a tendency to narrow the field of the divine operation to the realm of soteriology alone. God is seen chiefly, if not solely, as He who redeems men from sin. Much of our contemporary theology is strictly "salvation theology." Now there is, of course, a sense in which all theology must have to do with salvation; but this is true only if by salvation we mean the widest sort of rich and full, "abundant" life, which can come to men if and when they are rightly related, in the depths of their being, to the reality of God. Real life—what is meant in the Johannine writings by "eternal life"—is life that is lived in a conscious and obedient relationship to God whose sons we are; any life which is less than that is truncated, partial, and defective. But all too often, the kind of salvation which is in view is restricted to man's extrication from sin, whether by some action of God which "accounts" him righteous while he is still in sin or by some power which works through him to conquer the sin that reigns in his members. Obviously this is part, and in certain respects the central part, of the Christian Gospel; it is the proclamation of truth that even though we are in and of ourselves unacceptable, God in His mercy accepts us, counts us for His own, and works in us to accomplish our full freedom from sin. But surely there is more to the Christian view of God than this. And one of the greatest of the neo-orthodox theologians, Karl Barth himself, has seen this. Surely few contemporaries are more insistent upon man's sinfulness, and upon man's inability to extricate himself from that sinfulness, than Barth; yet it is noteworthy that his many-volumed *Kirchliche Dogmatik* includes section after section in which God's relationship to His world through creation and through the continued sustaining in creation of that which He has made is given strong emphasis.

But even Barth does not seem quite ready to have that generous recognition of the universality of the divine operation set apart from the narrowly soteriological and the wider range of the religious. It is probable that his rejection of the concept of general revelation, or at least his minimizing of this concept when it deals with that which is outside Scripture, and his unwillingness to invoke metaphysical thought and scientific discovery as contributory to our understanding of God and the world's relationship to God, are responsible for this failure in his thought. Yet in one sense his notion of the divine *incognito* might be the means to a wonderfully expanded view of the relationship of God to the world and to men in the world.

As we suggested in the last chapter, God must be concerned with much that is not strictly related to man's salvation, even with much that is not even religious. He is the Lord of the whole creation; and it ought to be part of the task of Christian thought to claim that whole creation for Him. Not that He is found in every area under His "proper" name of God; He is the ground of being, the Reality in all realities, the source and creative energy of the world. He is *incognito* wherever men are brought into the presence of that which is the token of what Paul Tillich has called their "ultimate concern." In all goodness, He is the Real Good; in all truth, He is the final Truth; in all beauty, He is the Supreme Excellence; in all loving, He is the Love which moves secretly yet compellingly. It is this kind of universal and pervasive presence and operation of God which we wish to urge as the only adequate portrayal of Him who is also our Lord and Sovereign Ruler.

Such a cosmic sweep for the meaning of deity redeems us from a trivial religiosity and gives our specifically Christian apprehension of God in the Man Christ Jesus a grandeur of setting and a richness of context that leads to increasing awe and wonder and to a deepened sense of the majesty and glory of the One who is our heavenly Father. Against that background, and only against it, can we rightly apprehend the Christian Gospel with its heart-shattering declaration that the "all-Great is the all-Loving too," and that, in the simple intimacies of human companionship with Jesus our human Brother, we are brought into immediate relationship with the God whose hand is over all His works.

V

THE INCARNATE CHRIST

THE discussion of the relation of God to His creation, with which the last chapter was concerned, might just as well have used, for an example, the principles and practice of prayer. For here, too, we discover that the consistent common sense of Christian thought has understood the meaning of prayer and the techniques that are employed in it, in a fashion which is much closer to the view of prayer that seems right in a world, such as our own age envisages, than the popular notion that prayer is a way of obtaining from God the things that we happen to desire. The real purpose of prayer is that our wills shall be brought into conformity with the will of God, through continued communion with Him; and the reason for our petitioning God for the particular things that we think we want is primarily that we shall have our desires purified, our motivations cleansed, and our relationship with Him strengthened. Unhappily, much of the understanding of prayer found in those who are supposedly instructed in these matters, as well as in those who are not within the circle of the Church's life, is essentially pagan. Here, once again, a genuinely theistic world view, such as the Christian Church has intended to defend, finds extraordinary confirmation from the results of scientific enquiry and the metaphysic that such results imply.

1

But we shall do much better to turn to the central assertion of the Christian message for a supreme illustration of the need for a restatement of our position. If we have come to see that the thought of a series of catastrophic intrusions is impossible in the kind of ordered world which both the Judaeo-Christian tradition and scientific research maintain, we shall be unable to talk of the Incarnation of God in Christ as if it were God's "coming" into a world from which otherwise He is absent. We must, of course, agree that the use of symbols of divine arrival, in a special sense, is apt for this peculiarly Christian belief in Christ; but, at the same time, we must recognize that here is a place where above all we dare not confuse symbolic aptness with literal predication. A conception of the Incarnation which expresses itself in talk of "a divine rescue expedition" or "the landing of a space-ship from another planet" (to cite two expressions found in recent popular Christian apologetic) is, in fact, in flat contradiction to the trinitarian theology of the Church. Later in this chapter we shall speak to this point. At the moment I should only insist on the sheer impossibility of such a view for any really profound understanding of the actual nature of things both religiously and scientifically.

I am myself convinced that one of the reasons for the rejection of the dogma of the Incarnation—using this phrase in the sense that I have intimated in earlier parts of this book—is that many otherwise Christian people are unable to accept a view which, as they think, makes nonsense of the whole of their experience. Often when one is told by some enquirer that he cannot accept the divinity of Jesus Christ, the appropriate response is, "what do you mean when you say 'divinity of Jesus Christ'?" For it is altogether likely that what the enquirer is rejecting is a view that one cannot oneself accept, and indeed a view that no thoughtful Christian has ever accepted. For example, it may be thought that to affirm our Lord's divinity is to look upon Him as an utterly unrelated wonder, having no connection with the rest of man's experience of God. Or it may be thought that He is divine in a sense that totally excludes His being human, or makes His humanity a truncated and partial reality. One of my old teachers used to say that "the heresy of the pious is Apollinarianism"—the heresy that denied to our Lord a real human mind. And the sermons of earnest preachers that I have heard over the past quarter century leads me to think that my old teacher was quite correct.

An illustration of the unintelligibility of the dogma of the Incarnation, when it is conceived as a divine intrusion, may be found in two recent books of Professor L. A. Reid. In each he rejects the notion that Jesus Christ is "God and Man," on the grounds that such a view would either make Jesus omniscient, or involve a mythical *kenosis* (emptying) which would be impossible for Godhead, or would imply a literal entrance of God into the world and so overthrow the humanity of Christ. Yet he can speak of Jesus as so possessed by "the Spirit of God," and of the union between God and Him as so marked and intimate, that He is our Lord and Saviour.

Should Dr. Reid be enabled to see that Incarnation is precisely a doctrine of *union,* that God is in every man (and also in all nature) united in some degree with His creation and working through it to reveal Himself and to accomplish His purposes, he would then be able to go on to see that *the* Incarnation is indeed both "the manner and mode of God's working in His creatures" (as Cardinal Bérulle put it); and also, since he insists that Jesus is unique, an unique Incarnation yet not cut off from the rest of God's revelation and activity. The suggestion, made by Professor A. E. Taylor, that our Lord's life is *at once* "everywhere creaturely," since He is a man, and "everywhere more than creaturely," since in Him the divine purpose shines through and controls the humanity, would fit well into this kind of statement of the Incarnation. And if for "the Spirit of God," we should substitute the *Logos,* or Word of God (as indeed Professor Reid is willing to say), the real meaning of the Christian insistence on Jesus as "Word made flesh," and therefore "truly God and truly man," would be asserted.

In fact, Professor Reid is opposing, not the doctrine of the Incarnation, but such distortions of it as, for example, Fr. Thornton's in *The Incarnate Lord,* in which the place of Jesus within the process of revelation and incarnation is denied in order to assert His finality—a question that we shall discuss in a later chapter. What is essential, if the thought forms available to men today are to be employed, is that *both* continuity of process *and* emergence of real novelty be preserved in any presentation of the doctrine. And we now turn to a way of stating the Incarnation that will preserve both these elements.

2

Dr. Paul Tillich has given us a phrase which is helpful in this connection, although I myself think that it minimizes (perhaps unintentionally) the element of *activity* in the Incarnation. He has spoken of the life of Jesus Christ as "transparent to the ground of being"; by this I gather that he means that in our Lord the nature of Reality, or in Tillich's idiom "the Unconditioned," is made manifest, so that through the conditions of Jesus' human life we can see and know the divine Reality in a vivid and compelling fashion.

This phrase has the value of relating Jesus to the whole process and movement of divine self-revelation, for Professor Tillich is clear that there are many points in the world order, as men experience it, that have the quality of "transparency." As I have indicated, I think that this notion has the defect of making the revelation of God in Christ too much a matter of *showing* and too little a matter of *acting*. I should prefer to describe the Incarnation as a unique focussing, for us men and for our wholeness, of a universal and pervasive divine *activity*. In that focal point, which is a focus of action, the total human life is made transparent to the divine Reality, and so Jesus becomes not only the place where God is most fully shown to us men in terms of our own human experience but also the place in which, as the center of a constellation of events, God is seen as most fully active for us in terms of our experience as men. *We could even say that our Lord's life is that place where human action in its highest reach is coincident with divine action in its most intensive form.* But it would be essential, in such a Christology, to make it clear that on any fundamentally theistic view the divine action must precede and make possible the human responsive action. This is by way of maintaining the important Christian conviction that Jesus Christ is not so much man achieving union with God as He is that One in whom God supremely establishes union with man. It is this insight which is behind the constant New Testament emphasis on the priority of God's act to man's response; and the New Testament emphasis rests back, of course, on the insistence of the Hebrew prophets that God is "prevenient" to all else, throughout the course of nature and history. This, incidentally, is the truth that is enshrined for us, so far as the person of Christ is concerned, in the credal symbol "conceived by the Holy Ghost, born of the Virgin Mary": God's action is prior to human response, yet that action, in one sense, "waits upon" the consent of man—"Be it unto me according to thy word." This special revelation of God in Christ, however, is to be related to the more general activity of God throughout His creation and more especially in human history and in human personality.

3

It is at this point that the patristic doctrine of the *Logos,* or Word of God, comes to our aid and relates the view which we are seeking to advance with some of the earliest and, as I think, best thought of the Christian Church. The *Logos* conception had its sources both in Greek thought, from which it found its way into Hellenistic Judaism, and in the Wisdom literature of the Old Testament, where it may also have been influenced by Greek thinking but where the fundamental idea seems to be a personalizing of the Wisdom, Will, Work, Hand, of God. Whatever its sources, this conception was employed in one way by the Johannine writer and in another way by St. Paul (for example, in Colossians), as a means by which the significance of Christ could best be expounded. And in some of the Fathers of the early Church we have a development of the view that seems to me to be of extraordinary value.

The *Logos,* or Word of God, signifies God in His self-expression. In Himself God remains a mysterious being: ultimate Reality is in Itself unfathomable by the human mind. But that is not all there is to God. On the contrary, God is ever expressive of Himself, and that expression, so genuinely a "part" of Himself, is the basic meaning of the whole creation. Indeed, we ought to capitalize the term, and speak of Expression as "with God" and as equally divine, being one with unoriginate God Himself. So the Fourth Evangelist presents the idea in the grand opening section of that "spiritual gospel." Now the Fathers, whose development of these significant points seems to me so important, speak of the Word as eternally "immanent" in Godhead—*Logos endiathetos.* By this they mean that it is ever and eternally the divine nature to be self-expressive, so much so that, in the mystery of the divine life, Self-Expression is an eternal mode of that life and being. But they also speak of the "uttered" Word—*Logos prophorikos.* The Word goes forth to be the agency or instrument of the creation. "The Heavenly Word, proceeding forth," yet never "leaving the Father's side" since the Word is eternally with God and is equally divine as God, is the means through which all things were made; that Word, who should be described indeed by a personal and not an impersonal pronoun, is the One who is at work in all creation, and also in all revelation and redemption.

In some instances, it appears that the Fathers suggested a "temporal utterance." But this is not always the case; and we may rightly reject such an idea and maintain that the Word is both eternally in God and eternally proceeding forth from God, and yet is at the same time "uttered" as the instrument through whom the worlds were made and by whose agency all revelation of the unmeasured Godhead occurs. The Fathers went beyond even this assertion, however. They believed that the Word of God was also present in and at work through men as the divine ground upon which all human life rests—*Logos spermatikos*. This is the "spermatic Word" of which Justin Martyr spoke when he declared that those who did not know Jesus Christ were still not without the Word of God, for all men must live by (and in and through) the Word. Hence we see that every good act, every loving thought and deed known to men, every trace of beauty in their lives, all that is right and true and fine, has its grounding in that Word who dwells in the secret heart of each man and who holds every human personality in being.

Finally—and here is the great and specifically Christian affirmation—the Fathers proclaimed the Word "enfleshed"—*Logos ensarkos*. In Jesus Christ the eternal Word of God is "en-manned"—*enanthroposanta,* and "we beheld his glory, the glory as of the unique Son of the Father, replete with the divine power and influence and favour, and replete too with the reality of God himself" (as we may translate the wonderful words of John I:14). And we must note that, by this, they mean that the Word is truly made *man,* with the total reality of human nature. Thus to say that Jesus is the "Word made flesh," or "the incarnate Word of God," is to say that in Him human nature in its fullness, with mind and body all compact, with "all things appertaining to the perfection of man's nature" (to quote, out of context, a phrase from Article IV of the *Thirty-nine Articles*), is the *organon,* or means of instrumental expression, for the very same Word of God who is the ground of all existence, including human existence, and who is also the agent of divine creation and revelation, while at the same time, He is the Self-Expressive Principle in Godhead itself—hence as divine as God because He is God. So we can say that in Jesus very God dwells in very man.

4

While preparing this chapter, I came across some words of William Scott Palmer, written nearly a half-century ago, which bring this conception into close relationship with ordinary human experience. Palmer writes:

We Christians know that the deep kinship of human spirits, their permeation of each other by mutual love and intuitive understanding, in which each interweaves his own mystery with the mystery of the

other, must give some clue to our relation everywhere, even with God. Holding this clue, we learn
that what we call our sonship in God must at least
mean the capacity of receiving him into ourselves
and penetrating into his desire for us. We begin to
see that we may know him as a divine yet human
will and character, becoming our own will and character. So God . . . may become visible in . . . man
. . . All that is needed is that the way be cleared by
the breaking-down of barriers set against the coming of God . . .

If a man never opposed God, if he were always
permeable to the divine influx, he would be God's
Son, wholly his, as a man amongst men. The manifestation of God would be local . . . in a little
place and stated time; God would be, as always,
infinitely beyond it, and beyond any truth it would
reveal; but he would be present there, he would be
revealed in the man, according to his measure as a
man. And that is the highest we can reach, the most
of God we can really know.[1]

My only criticism of this passage is that it is imperative here, as in the following quotation from the same
author, to emphasize that it is God who is prior to man;
and that the "breaking-down of barriers" is the work
of the Holy Spirit of God, through whom the way is

[1] William Scott Palmer, *Diary of a Modernist* (London: Edward
Arnold, 1910), pp. 174-177.

prepared for the permeation by God the Word of a human life, throughout the whole of its existence from conception onwards—an action which is in the divine purpose "before all time" and through the whole providentially ordered course of human history. This is the fulfilment which we see in Jesus Christ. The quotation continues:

[God] has always been thus expressed, in some degree; for his love is before and with all worlds, urgent in all men everywhere, conquering, invading, by his prevenient and sufficient grace, their blind or wilful resistance. And the fact that there are degrees in our resistance to his gift of himself, but none in the urgency of his desire to give; the fact that he is without variableness or shadow of turning, shows . . . that somewhere, at some time, and necessarily at a place and a time, he may well have found a human way unbarred and opened wide. That way, free from even the weak resistance of his saints, would give place to a new beginning upon earth, a difference not in degree but in kind—the difference between the unbroken whole of a proper human perfection, and the more or less of imperfection in other men. There God would show, at last, the way, the truth, and the life of man. There God, embracing finitude and growing in wisdom and statute, would become, at last, "manifest in the flesh" as a man whose kingdom should have no end. He would come among us unthwarted, seeking his own as man seeks man; endowed with the narrow but penetrating advantage of bodily approach, a halting yet intelligible speech for the eternal Word. So he, the God ever striving but hidden in each one of us, knocking always at the door of every heart, would also draw near to us from without, in a visible sacrament and by a love eloquent in the actual life of one man.

This is what Christians claim for Jesus Christ. I should myself wish to emphasize, in this admirable quotation from Palmer, that it is not sin alone ("resistance") which explains why incarnation is only potential in the race (or at best intimated and adumbrated) until *the* Incarnation occurs; rather, I think, it is once again the divine plan and purpose which in a supreme sense providentially ordered all things, so that the emergence of the life "prepared for God's Word" is itself the operation of the Holy Spirit, whether through normal human intercourse or in some other way. And I should wish to prescind from a discussion of "differences of degree" and "difference of kind" because, as it seems to me, this introduces logical problems that are not only insoluble but (as William Temple noted in *Christus Veritas*) fundamentally absurd.

But with these comments I believe that Palmer has stated, in language which is both right in carrying on the Patristic Christology already outlined and right also in speaking intelligibly to modern man, that which is the heart of the Christian message. It is my conviction that some such approach to the Incarnation will make sense of the whole witness of Christian experience stemming from the evangelical record, and also be able to take into account the orderliness and self-consistency of the divine operation in nature, in history, and in human experience, —an orderliness which, as I have said, seems to me not only disclosed by modern study and thought but also implicit in the whole Judaeo-Christian tradition.

5

Furthermore, such an approach is able to reckon with the problem that "science-fiction," and its more serious counterpart, the contemporary interest in the exploration of space and in the possibility of life on other planets, poses for the modern Christian apologist. And this leads me to a discussion of the question mentioned earlier— that the Christian epic seems too small for the vastly expanded universe which we now know. I wish to devote the remainder of this chapter to a consideration of this problem as it is put to us by "science-fiction," for in my experience on college campuses and in the "schools of religion" of many parishes I have discovered that it has become very real and very difficult for many who would accept the Christian faith.

Let me get at the point by a bit of autobiography. For one whose chief relaxation is the reading of detective novels—why is this a hobby of theologians?—it is a dreadful thing to find oneself on a long trip without some such book. But it was worse when I found myself, not many months ago, on a long train ride with nothing to read. So I stopped at the newsstand and looked for a book. All I could find was "science-fiction." I had never read much of this kind of thing, although I had struggled through Mr. C. S. Lewis's tales, such as *Perelandra* and *Out of the Silent Planet,* and not found them much to my liking, and had attempted, but not gone far with, Mr. Charles Williams's novels. I had, as it happens, rejected this particular kind of Christian apologetic. But the only book that I could pick up on the newsstand was a collection of short stories gathered from *Galaxy,* a "science-fiction" journal. I accepted my fate, purchased the book, and began to read. The stories introduced me to what is obviously an increasingly popular kind of writing and they had a certain fascination if one made allowance for the exaggeration and the violence that made at first the experience of reading so exasperating.

And then, a short time afterward, I was sent a book that discussed in highly technical terms the relation of modern scientific cosmology to Christian theism. In the closing chapter of this volume the author, the late Dr. E. A. Milne, distinguished Oxford scientist, raised the question of the salvation of inhabitants of distant planets, if inhabitants there be on these planets. He was, for himself, convinced that the earth is not the only inhabited portion of the cosmos; he believed that some form of life, in whatever degree of development and whatever form of physical manifestation, is likely to be present in many other planets. As a Christian, Dr. Milne was concerned with the question of the knowledge of God and the possibility of salvation which might be available to such living beings.

His own solution of the problem was a very "science-fiction" one. He felt it possible that the Christian Gospel might some day be brought to such living beings when we have conquered space. One had a picture of missionaries commissioned to preach on Mars or Venus or some remote star in one of the other galaxies. And it was only in this fashion that Dr. Milne could envisage salvation for those planets which had not known God in Jesus Christ.

It is not only in such relatively advanced theoretical discussion as that by this English scientist that the question which he raises is of concern and interest. Conversation with college students and others has shown that one unexpected result of the popular "science-fiction" point of view, as well as of the present serious consideration of interplanetary communication, is a new problem for Christian theology and apologetics. Some of the attempts to solve the problem, often found in quite valuable writers, represent what is in effect a retreat from a solution. It is said that this world is the only certainly inhabited planet and that, therefore, we need not even concern ourselves with the question. Certain writers are even prepared to stake everything on the assumed fact that intelligent life is found only on earth; it is evidently thought by them that the Christian position falls to the ground if it is admitted that there is a possibility of other inhabited planets.

6

The real solution of the problem is found in a more profound understanding of the Christian affirmations about the Trinity and the Incarnation. For us, on this planet, there can be no doubt that the historical event of the life, death, and resurrection of Jesus Christ is the central moment, the crucial point, in the God-man relationship. But note what is asserted in Christian theology about Jesus Christ. He is said to be the incarnation of the Word of God; in Him the Second Person of the Blessed Trinity was united with human nature in as intimate and direct a way as is possible for man. But it is not asserted that God is operative only in Jesus Christ; He is definitive, but not exhaustive, in the whole relationship of God with His human children. God has "nowhere left himself without witness"; "in him we live and move and have our being." And the Word, the Second Person of the Trinity, is that same Word "by whom all things were made." The Word, in developed Trinitarian theology, is the Self-Expressive Principle in God; through the agency of the Word God created and creates. Are we not then justified in going on to say that it is also through the Word, the Self-Expressive Principle in God, that all revelation and all redemption occur? In fact, we seem obliged to say just this, since it is by the Word made flesh in Jesus of Nazareth, accepted as Christ, that we know of this revealing and redeeming work in a vivid and vital way.

It may not be entirely clear what the writer of the Fourth Gospel meant to imply by his sentence about the Word's being "in the world," being "the light" because He was "the life" of men. But it is certainly not impossible to read, as we have already done in this chapter, the whole of the first fourteen verses of St. John as a way of saying that the Self-Expressive Principle in Godhead is the agent both of creation and revelation, wherever and however these may occur. Nor is it impossible to claim that the writer of that Gospel was above all concerned to maintain and defend the cosmic reality of that Word, who, among many other things, was for us *men* and for *our* salvation en-manned in Jesus.

If we take this as our point of departure, there is no theological objection to the belief that the same Word, who for our human redemption was made flesh in Palestine two thousand years ago, can and does act as the agent of redemption for other intelligent species which may exist elsewhere in the universe. There is no reason to doubt that He who became *man* for our planet, could become Martian for those who live on that planet, and so with any other world in which life reaches the point where conscious God-relationship is a possibility. How such a revelation and redemption would be effected we cannot know. The sort of incarnate action which might be found elsewhere than on this earth we could not fathom, at least in our present phase of existence. But there is

100

no reason to assume that it is impossible or unlikely.

The point is that for the Christian who has seen that even in this world all the good and saving forces known to men are really the operation of the Word, while all the responding and accepting of these forces by men is the work of the Holy Spirit, the thought that these operations and workings may extend far beyond this planet is not disturbing but rather wonderfully enriching and capable of moving to deeper worship and praise for the marvellous ways of God. It is conceivable that the inhabitants of some planets, if there be any such inhabitants, may not have fallen into some equivalent of human sin. But even there, we need not regard the work of God in Christ as *solely* a remedy for sin. We ought to be prepared to accept something like the Scotist notion that the Incarnation would have occurred had man not sinned, since God would wish to unite His human creatures with Him as intimately and directly as the Incarnation implies. Thus we can believe that the sinless (if they be such) but intelligent beings who may exist elsewhere in the creation still can know union with God, according to their way of existence; and so they could be united with us in response to the ever-active, ever-loving Reality who made them and us.

Nor do we have any idea of the different stages of development that such creatures may have reached. Some of them may have gone far beyond us in spiritual qualities; others may be far below us. But each and all of them would still be related to the same God, through

101

the agency of the same Self-Expressive Principle in God, responding to that action through the same Responding Power. In other words, God the Father, God the Son, and God the Holy Ghost would be as much a reality for them, under their special conditions, as He is for us under ours.

7

Admittedly all of this is speculation. We do not *know* anything about other planets, at least at the moment, beyond that which science can tell us of their physical and chemical properties and the *possibilities* of life emerging from these combinations. But at least this speculation is of a sort which is directly in line with a whole stream of theological thought; and it has the value of delivering us from a needless concern for the religious life of whatever other intelligent beings may exist, while at the same time it expands our view of the Christian religion and shows us that our God is much more than the God of one particular planet and that our particular planet need not be the center of everything.

Yet, with all this said, it must also be said that for us men, for our knowledge of God, and for our entrance upon the way of wholeness which is the way of salvation, all that is necessary has been done for us in Jesus Christ. For us He is the focus of God's revelation as He is the focus of God's redemption of men. And it may be that one day, when we are admitted to the unveiled presence of God, we shall join with many other creatures, from

102

many other planets, as well as with angels and archangels and all the company of heaven, in praising our Maker for His wonderfully various, yet always loving, work for those whom He has created.

Alice Meynell once wrote a remarkable poem called "Christ in the Universe." She spoke of the fact that it is through

> the message to the Maid, the human birth,
> The lesson, and the Young Man Crucified[2]

that *we* have been told the "terrible, frightened, shamefast, whispered, sweet, heart-shattering secret of God's way with us." But she went on to speculate that "in the immensities" we may learn of what God has done elsewhere, when

> In our turn, we show to them a Man.

[2] Alice Meynell, "Christ in the Universe," from *Collected Poems of Alice Meynell* (New York: Charles Scribner's Sons, 1923), p. 92.

VI

BIBLICAL RELIGION
AND BIBLICAL THEOLOGY

T HE title of this chapter is an indication of its *tendenz*.
In the face of a new situation in the world of biblical
study, it is my intention to maintain that (a) the religion
of the Bible is central and normative in Christian faith
and life; (b) the theology which emerges from a study
of the Bible is indicative of the proper line of development in the intellectual statement of that faith and
life; but (c) the theology of the Bible as found therein
in express terminology and statement is not to be taken
as *exclusively* determinative of all properly Christian
theological faith and life.

It has been characteristic of many biblical students in

many quarters during the past few decades that no specifically theological interest should be allowed to obtrude
itself into their study, lest (as they thought) objectivity
be lost in the process. Naturally the theologians welcome the change in atmosphere which makes it possible
to have a theological treatment of the Holy Scriptures
and their significance. But one theologian at least is a
little concerned lest, in the present rush towards a
deepened theological interest in Scripture, there shall
come about an unhappy and, indeed, a dangerous loss of
objectivity, on the one hand, and an erroneous attitude
towards the place of the Bible in Christian faith and life,
on the other.

We have witnessed on the continent of Europe and in
America and Britain, the appearance of what is called
"biblical theology." It is all the fashion nowadays to
speak of the Bible as pre-eminently the "theological"
book. Appeal is made not to sheer history nor to the
reconstructed text nor to the "findings" of biblical science,
but rather to the theological stress, the doctrinal teaching, the dogma expressly stated, in the Sacred Book.
It is hardly necessary for me to recount the story of
"how this came about." And I should be the last person
to decry the new movement which has almost entirely
conquered European and English biblical study and is
making its influence felt very strongly in our own country. But when I read books in which the author feels
that it is quite irrelevant to any understanding of the
religious meaning of, say, the Fourth Gospel, whether

that work was written by one man or another, thereby disregarding or minimizing many years of sound and scholarly work that has shown us quite plainly that the author of the Fourth Gospel was certainly not the disciple who leaned on Jesus' breast; or studies in which the Old Testament is used as a storehouse for Christian dogmatic theology with no attention to, or interest in, its specific illustration of the development of Judaism in all its richness and variety, thereby disregarding or minimizing the work of critics from Wellhausen down to the present; or books in which "the unity of the New Testament" is asserted without due appreciation of the remarkable growth of doctrinal understanding and presentation in the several strata, thereby disregarding or minimizing all that the last fifty years of synoptic criticism, not to mention the minute analysis of the rest of the New Testament, has revealed to us; when, I say, I come across these things, I cannot but feel that we are faced by a danger which is not so obvious as it might be, precisely because there is so much to be said for the emphasis that is being laid upon the theological and doctrinal side of the matter.

1

Perhaps the best method in which my own positive views may be presented is by proceeding, in a somewhat personal vein, to speak of the attitude of one theologian to the whole area of biblical study. And the first thing that I should wish to say as a theologian is that we are, all of us, greatly indebted to historical criticism, not to speak of textual criticism, for our present grasp of the development of Jewish religion and the emergence of Christianity. It is utterly impossible ever to return to the naive fundamentalism of an earlier day; we should be grateful for that. The studies in Old Testament, by which in recent years we can discern the development of the "J" material, for example, seem to me to be of first importance. The investigation into the relationship between Judaism and the surrounding religious cultures as well as the aboriginal Canaanitish culture has given us results which have deep theological interest and value. The form-critics have contributed enormously to the comprehension which we may now claim to possess as to the way in which the initial impetus of Christian faith grew, and altered as it grew. The Pauline studies that have appeared in recent years are useful in assisting us in the task of reconstructing the response made by this formative theological mind of primitive Christianity to the tradition about Jesus as he had received it. So one might go over the whole list; theological study is bound to be different these days because of that which has been done in the field of biblical study.

One illustration will perhaps suffice. In rethinking the whole question of the Christian conception of "heaven and hell," it has been borne in upon me that no longer can any of us make those easy appeals to the sayings of Jesus, to the intimations of the prophets, to the chance remarks of St. Paul and others, which characterized an older theological approach. We must find another way, not a less desirable one but a more desirable one—more desirable because new truth has come to us from biblical study, and our statement of the essential Christian position must be quite different in method, although not necessarily entirely different in result.

There can be little doubt, then, that the work of the critics has been of enormous help to us all. But it would be absurd to say that any critic, whether he be an old-fashioned synoptic critic or a new-fangled form-critic, ever really does what he so often thinks he is doing. He is never able, for instance, to give us an utterly unbiased picture of the historical Jesus. For in the work of any and every critic, there is inevitably an element of interpretation, as there must also be a series of presuppositions, usually concealed even from the critic himself. It is this fact that led George Tyrrell to make his famous remark about the older "liberal" critics: they looked into a deep well, he said, and saw at the bottom what they thought was the historical Jesus, but what in truth was their own reflection. It is largely by way of reaction from this dangerous consequence of critical study, I suppose, that the revolt towards a theological interpretation of the Bible came about.

2

Much of the revived biblical theology is, in my belief, essentially a return to a pre-critical position. Let me put this as strongly as I can and, therefore, perhaps somewhat unjustly. My illustration will be the theology of St. Paul. It is important to know what St. Paul believed, how his theology is articulated and finally stated. What is more important is the religion which St. Paul possessed, or better which possessed him. The particular forms and words which he used are of value to us in that they are *his* forms and words, used by him to express so far as he could his dominant conviction that in Jesus Christ God had visited and redeemed His people. Again, it is important to know what elements entered into St. Paul's belief and how this was modified by his contact with non-Jewish circles; it is much more important to know that he was using any and every experience to "get across" his supreme conviction about life in terms of Jesus Christ. But in our anxiety to stress the latter, it is unwise and dangerous to overlook the former, since the only way in which we know anything at all about St. Paul's dominant conviction is through his particular set of thought-forms and ideas.

Similarly, I do not myself believe that the Messianic conception, *as such,* has an enduring significance in the modern world. It is extraordinarily important in its Jewish context; it may have been in the mind of Jesus Himself as descriptive of His own person, although I am inclined to doubt it. What is fundamental is that Jesus is that One, who was so interpreted in Jewish terms, because it was thought that He could only adequately be described in those terms for those days. But the Church went on to see that He could *not* in fact adequately be so described and went on to use other terms, such as *Logos,* and finally called Him Very God dwelling in Very Man. Yet it is imperative that the fullest exploration of the biblical terms be carried on, since it is only in those terms and in that context that we have any knowledge of the historic Jesus Himself and of that impact which He made upon history which has led to the full Christian affirmations about Him.

You will now see why I am sure that the dilemma often proposed—historical *or* interpretative study of the Bible —is a false dilemma. We need both. It is absolutely essential that we have the most thoroughgoing investigation of the data of Holy Scripture, in the light of our wider secular knowledge of the periods and areas that are involved and with the use of every critical tool that is available and susceptible of our employment. On the other hand, we shall never hope to understand the Bible as other than a collection of interesting religious speculations and a few, not too well authenticated, facts if we do not bring to this study the additional reality of our own Christian appurtenance. In this sense only a Christian can understand the Bible. Yet we shall be obliged to add that the understanding of the Bible is never complete when it is strictly and solely theological, without reference to that historical rootedness upon which Jewish and Christian religions do in fact rest.

3

Since, in my own work, my special interest has been the doctrine of Christ, I can best show my own method by referring to that area of biblical study. Let us grant that we have accepted the conclusions of the form-critics when they assert that the Gospels are all of a piece in that they are interpretative presentations, in terms of the life-situations of the primitive Church, of the figure of Jesus. Now it is, of course, possible to take an extremely sceptical position, saying that since all we know of Jesus is through the tradition of the primitive community, we have only a "cult-figure." In that case, Christianity is no longer interesting excepting as a curious historical phenomenon. Or we can follow the particular biblical theologians who would dismiss the historical quest and rest content with the faith of the Church as expressed in the New Testament. But we may also take the position of those who would say, as I myself should say, that the religion which is portrayed in the New Testament is so vital, so significant, so impelling, that it must point to an historic grounding, such as is given to us in the evangelical story. It is true that we know this figure only through the faith of the primitive community; it is true that history is not without interpretation. But it is possible to maintain that view precisely because Christianity is a religion which is, by its very nature, involved in history; and because history by its very nature is known to us only through interpretation

112

of fact, we have here not an outlandish or absurd approach, but a natural and right one. We only know the historical Jesus through the Christ of faith, even if that faith be the primitive and unformed faith reflected in much of the New Testament. On the other hand, we only have the Christ of Christian faith if we can confidently affirm that there is some historical residuum, some nucleus of fact, some "happenedness" (in von Hügel's phrase), which will account for the emergence of the faith which the New Testament, in varying fashion, presents to us. Yet that faith is not tied down to the New Testament terms or ideas; it can—it historically *did*—develop and expand. Yet it was developed and expanded in a straight line. In that sense the theology implied and sometimes stated in the New Testament is normative; but it is not confining nor exclusive.

4

It is obvious, therefore, that "other grounds" must be given for the Christian position than merely biblical ones. These are life in fellowship with the Church, shared with Christian brethren, nourished by the sacraments and deepened by prayer, expressed in action and constantly related to the ultimate reality of God in terms of the Church's traditional affirmation that Reality was supremely en-manned for our wholeness and health, made flesh and dwelling amongst us, in a Man. If this is the truth of my life, I cannot call it a lie in fact. In other words, we must speak "confessionally," as Protestant writers put it; for me it is more natural to say that we must speak "as of the Church." Other considerations than the biblical do and must enter into one's religion. And other considerations than the critical and historical must enter into one's estimate of the critical and historical questions. But they cannot and must not lead to a neglect or minimizing of the problems to which critical and historical study leads, nor to a disregarding of the conclusions of that study.

Perhaps this can be put yet more personally and, thereby, more clearly. No consideration of which I am aware has ever prevented me from following through to the end any and every consequence of the study of the Bible. The reason for this is, presumably, that my faith is not in the Bible but in the God of whom the Bible speaks and whose saving acts, as the Christian Church sees them, are related in the Sacred Text. My faith in God, furthermore, is a faith held in the Church's fellowship, sustaining me and establishing me in the life in Christ which *is* Christianity. So I approach the Bible free to study it critically, free also to see its imperfections, free to use it and profit by it, but free also to recognize that the Christian position, although rooted and grounded therein, is bigger than the Bible, bigger even than the theology of the Bible and, perhaps in some instances, other than the theology which the Bible suggests. I suppose that this is a variant of Catholic Modernism. In any case, it makes it possible for me to maintain the thesis with which I started: The religion of the Bible is

114

central and normative in Christian life, while its theology is indicative of the true line of Christian development; yet it must be studied critically and historically, thoroughly and unflinchingly, so that the religion which lives at the heart of Christianity may continue to flourish and the theology which expresses that religion in dogmatic terms may be alert and vital, as well as historically continuous with the original response made by the primitive Church to the total fact of Christ.

VII

THE TASK OF CHRISTIAN SELF-CRITICISM

Our concern hitherto has been primarily with intellectual difficulties encountered in our effort as preachers and teachers to "get our message across." It has been necessary to discuss these intellectual problems, for a faith that lacks a sound theological basis can have no enduring significance. Doctrine has sometimes been given a bad name; but a religion without doctrine would be at the mercy of emotion and fancy. Indeed, it is not so much doctrine with which we ought to be concerned, as it is with dogma, which has an even worse reputation in some quarters. But that reputation has been earned not by the fact of dogma itself but by the way in which some theologians have handled the subject. Dogma means only the accepted and agreed beliefs, in their intellectually determined statement, upon which the Christian life itself depends. The claim that God is in Christ, in a fashion which is so real and so focal that Christ may rightly be seen as Lord, necessarily finds expression in a dogma concerning who Christ is and what He has done and still does for men. The formal wording of the dogma may change from time to time, as men's understanding of the world changes the setting in which they must inevitably place Christ; but the essential truth which is being stated remains constant so long as Christianity itself remains a workable religion for men.

Doctrine, in a general sense, is the theological expression of the Christian faith; but doctrines, in particular, are really secondary to dogma. They are concerned with systematizings, theologies, orderings of belief, and the like; and they naturally vary from Christian theologian to Christian theologian. Even so, the theological enterprise is inevitable in the Christian Church. It is only when we forget that *pectus facit theologum*—that the living faith which dwells in men's hearts and is summarily stated in the few utterly essential Christian dogmas creates the theologian and must govern all of his work—that theology becomes a sterile activity and the theologian a mere antiquarian or speculative thinker without vital relationship to an on-going religious concern.

Yet I must emphasize that *Christianity is primarily a life to be lived and not a set of theories and speculations.*

It is certainly not primarily a theology, although (as I have said) I for one am convinced that, without a sound theology and one that is defensible not only by the standard of evangelical truth to which the Church must always return but also by the standard of reason in its widest and richest sense, the Christian life cannot really be lived at all. But Christianity is, at heart, a life that is lived in commitment and expressed in worship. It is, above all, a life that is lived in intimate relationship with Reality apprehended in Christ. It is related to reality, with a lower-case "r," in the sense that it is concerned with, and has its constant relevance to, the real facts of life, of history, of nature, as men know and experience them in all their variety and in all their richness. It is related to Reality, with an upper-case "R," in the sense that it is not a matter of values or ideals but of God, who is the ground of all existence and the inescapable *There* with whom every man has to do. That is why sentimentality, easy ecclesiasticism and "churchiness," and a narrowly "religious" outlook which fails to see God in the so-called "secular" realms of life, or tries to reduce these realms to the specifically "religious," are impossible for the sensitive and honest Christian thinker.

1

The setting for the whole theological enterprise is the Church as the worshipping community. In our own day the liturgical movement is re-asserting the centrality of worship and the way in which through the great liturgical action of the Church the Christian is made a living member of the community of faith. But it must also be said that all of our attempts to state, in intellectually adequate and compelling terms, the meaning of our faith have their real source in the adoration of God in Christ through the Spirit. It is this adoration that matters above all. We shall never hope to grasp the deepest meaning of Christianity unless we see it as a faith which is expressed in worship and which leads to worship, as it also springs from the worship called forth from us as we are brought into relationship with Jesus Christ.

Furthermore, that faith with its profound grounding in worship must have for its goal the development in men of what traditional theology has called "the life in grace." A Christian is one who believes in the Christian way and who worships in the Christian way; he is also one whose life is "in Christ." The charity of God, spread abroad in our hearts through the Spirit given us in Christ, is the secret of Christian living; and with it are coupled the humility which recognizes our human creatureliness and the courage which sends us forth to reflect the Spirit of Christ in the affairs of daily life. Thus worship and life are the implementation of faith; while faith is the link which binds the adoration of the mystery of God (as He has made Himself known in the event of Christ) and the new and "en-Christed" behavior of Christians with their brethren.

I have said all this because there is sometimes the danger, to which Hastings Rashdall made reference over fifty years ago in the final chapter of his noble book *Christus in Ecclesia,* that those who wish a theology which is liberal in the best sense may be thought to neglect the devotional riches and the personal and social implications of the Christian tradition. On the contrary, as Rashdall said, we must "endeavour to identify ourselves as intimately as we may be allowed to do with the tradition of reverent devotion and corporate activity, which is the happy heritage of [the Church]." He counseled:

> Let us identify ourselves as much as we possibly can with the religious life and the practical activities around us, while we strive to cultivate in ourselves, and to communicate to others, that spirit of free enquiry and open-mindedness which is, no less than zeal and devotional fervour, a manifestation of the Spirit of God.[1]

How this is made possible, in a unique sort of way, in the Anglican Communion's inclusive apprehension of the Christian faith, will be the subject of our concluding chapter.

2

Having said this, I wish to discuss the problem of the restatement of the Christian message in a somewhat dif-

[1] Hastings Rashdall, *Christus in Ecclesia* (Edinburgh: T. and T. Clark, 1912), p. 364. Used by permission of the publisher.

ferent fashion from our earlier treatment, although with some necessary repetition of ideas.

On every side, these days, we hear of the need for a return to, or revival of, religious faith. It is not only the literary leaders of our day, many of whom have been converted in recent years to the Christian Church in one or other of its branches, who tell us that such a return is the only alternative to destruction; nor is it the statesmen and experts on public affairs. Almost everywhere one turns, when conversation has penetrated beneath the superficialities, one discovers that quite ordinary men and women recognize this truth. They want to "believe in something"; they feel the terrible need for "some real security" which they readily agree only a religious faith can offer. They are no longer in the cynical mood so well described by the English phrase, "I couldn't care less." In fact, large numbers of our fellowmen are "ripe" for faith.

That on the one hand. And on the other, the apparent impossibility for many of them—and often, these are the most desirous to believe—of the Christian religion as they understand it. For some reason, as we have said, the organized churches do not seem able to "get their message across." Or if they do, the message does not make the sort of appeal that it should. All the statistics which show that church membership in America is slightly ahead of the growth of population will not compensate for the fact that for large numbers of wistful and needy men and women, the Christian faith simply does not make sense, nor can they see their way clear to accept it.

It is very easy to say that this has ever been so. We know that there is an "offense" about authentic Christianity which will inevitably put men off, unless they are ready and willing to make an act of humble submission. The worldly, the sensuous, the selfish and wilful must always find that the Christian Gospel is a scandal to them. And scandal it should be. But the difficulty is not here. For it is frequently precisely the men and women that are not worldly, not sensuous, not selfish and wilful, who wish desperately to believe, but who find themselves unable to take the step.

3

With our revival of orthodox Christianity, in the classical sense of that phrase, our theologians have helped us to see much about man that we had for many years failed to recognize. We know now about man's sinfulness; we have had, if anything, an overdose of teaching and preaching about original sin, about man's distorted and twisted nature, about his tendency to lord it over the creation. All of this we must take into account, for it is true. And the interesting fact is that the very people who are outside the Christian Church are often most ready to accept this. Arthur Schlesinger, Jr., and Lionel Trilling, whom we have already mentioned, as well as Arthur Koestler and others, have made this clear enough to us. But they do not accept the Gospel of man's redemption, which alone could deliver them from the oppressing sense of human evil and man's impotence in the face of life's inexorable demands. So we are forced back to our earlier question: why is this? why does not the Christian Gospel make the appeal which it should make to men who are ready to acknowledge that "they have done those things which they ought not to have done, and left undone those things which they ought to have done, and there is no health in them"?

There are, of course, many explanations which could be given for this strange phenomenon. In this book, I am seeking to explore only one of these explanations; and I have realized that the suggestions which I make will, to many of my readers, savour of the "old-fashioned liberalism" or the "minimizing modernism," from which neo-orthodoxy is supposed to have delivered us. One explanation, then, is that Christianity as it is often preached, taught, expounded, defended, is to many moderns simply incredible on the ground that it makes nonsense of the rest of their experience and their knowledge of the world in which we live. This is by no means the only reason for the failure of the faith to make its appeal; but I, for one, remain convinced that it is a major reason.

Nor am I referring to outlandish fundamentalist preaching of Christianity. That sort of thing, making its appeal to certain types of mind and especially to those of slight education, will always put off the men and women who are actually living in the twentieth century, with its particular understanding of the world derived from science and the other knowledge of our time. Neither do I refer to Roman Catholicism, which, with its tight authoritarianism, also makes its appeal to those who wish and, therefore, seek a totalitarianism of the mind and spirit. I am talking about the kind of Christianity which is found in the ordinary run-of-the-mill parish—since I am an Episcopalian, shall I say of the Episcopal Church? —which is neither sheerly authoritarian, on the one hand, nor crudely fundamentalist, on the other.

There are, I believe, at least three areas where the Christian claim seems incredible to the sort of person we are discussing—the moderately well-educated, well-informed, thoughtful person whom we all know so well. These areas could be described as follows: The claim to absolute truth; the claim that the Christian way alone is the way to salvation; and the claim that Christianity is only to be accepted in terms of a sheerly "miraculous" world view. It is my purpose to say something about each of these three, although I have already discussed a variation of the triad in the second chapter. Here, however, we approach the subject in a new way.

4

Modern men and women, when they have not permitted themselves to be enamoured of the totalitarian faiths such as communism or Romanism, are unwilling to allow that any single man, or any group of men, can ever have an exhaustive and complete knowledge. They are suspicious of "absolutes." We do not need to blame John Dewey and the pragmatists for this distrust; it is a simple fact of the modern mind, which precisely because it grasps something of the vastness of creation, both in duration and extent, cannot concede that any man, or group of men, could have absolute knowledge about the mystery. Now as a matter of fact, authentic Christianity has never really made this claim, despite the many representatives of the Church who have talked as if it did. Christianity has asserted that there is indeed an absolute commitment that men must make on those matters which (as Paul Tillich has taught us to say) are their "ultimate concern." It has never asserted that it possessed a complete knowledge of the mystery of life. "The light shineth in darkness"; and although the darkness "does not overcome it," yet there are vast areas concerning which Christianity has no more genuine information than any other philosophy or perspective. In a profound sense, Christianity has always been pragmatic; it has said that in the light of a central affirmation, accepted with the whole being of the believer, illumination is given sufficient for us to walk with confidence and dignity in the world into which we have been thrust, while on the other hand there is provided, from that same affirmation, a dynamic which makes it possible for us to live in scorn of consequence, with courage and hope.

A proper humility in the presentation of the Christian affirmation; the insistence that this is indeed a "faith" and not "knowledge"; the readiness to learn from any and every human enterprise more about the world in which we live—all of this is requisite if the Christian proclamation is to make any appeal to men and women who are so deeply conscious of the mystery of existence and the absurdity of claims to absolute and exhaustive knowledge.

But there is something to be said on the other side. Sometimes we are all too ready to declare the mystery sooner than we need. Human reason can do something, if not very much, to lighten our path. The Christian Church does no service to men when it takes refuge in a mystery where, in fact, a little study would provide the information we need. That is why we should welcome, and let it be widely known that we welcome, the work of the scientists and others who are discovering so much that is important and useful about the world, about human life, about man's motivations and the dynamics of his personality. In fact, what we need is the proclamation of a final commitment, coupled with a humility which makes no claims to absolutes *and* with a generosity of spirit which gladly accepts truth from whatever quarter it may come.

It is especially in respect to the theology of the Church that this attitude needs cultivation. The theology of the Church is not an exact statement of truth, nor even an exact statement of the Gospel; it is an attempt to work out, with humility and modesty, such an articulated statement of the content of the *Gospel,* in relation to the pervasive activity of God in His creation, as shall express for thoughtful men the meaning of the faith by which they live. *Dogmas are not revealed, nor are they of the*

127

nature of inevitable logical deductions from the facts of revelation; they are an expression, symbolic in nature and to be understood much more aesthetically than scientifically, of the vision granted us through the action of God in nature and history. When they are seen in this way, they no longer give unnecessary offense to men who know perfectly well the absurdity and presumption of the claim to have God and His ways "taped" and set forth in human words with precise scientific accuracy.

5

Or take the supposed claim that Christianity is the only way by which salvation is offered to men. In the first place, what do we mean by "salvation"? Is it not all too frequently presented as a kind of extrication from the world; or perhaps as guarantee of secure possession of heavenly bliss? And would it not be wiser if we sought to show that both etymologically and also for a sound theology "salvation" means health, wholeness of life, good enough to enjoy here and now, and good enough to last, through the vicissitudes of mundane existence and the finality of death, unto an eternal enjoyment of God? But granted this, why should we claim that it is only in Christianity that men can find such wholeness of life, such health? The whole theological tradition of the eternal Word of God, ever moving out from the heart of Deity and ever operative in the creation; the Word of God "by whom all things were made," as the Nicene Creed puts it; the Word of God who is the "ground" of all creaturely existence and supremely of human life; the Word of God who, among all the other things that He is ever doing, has focussed His operation in the human life of Jesus of Nazareth, in whom He dwelt "as a Son," incarnate "for us men and for our salvation"—this whole tradition, properly understood and properly proclaimed, guarantees both the reality of all "saving experiences," wherever they may be found—under whatever religious name or through whatever secular incognito—and also the centrality and definitiveness of that which was "determined, dared and done" in the Lord Jesus Christ.

The new orthodoxy, in certain of its representatives, has entirely forgotten or completely rejected this long tradition. And by so doing, it may have sharpened for some the decisiveness of the Christian claim, but it has much more certainly denied the cosmic sweep of the divine action and made Christianity a parochial and narrow thing. And by assuming that all of man's seeking and yearning has met answer in Christ alone, it has turned God into a niggardly Deity, forgetting that His "nature and property is *always* to have mercy and to forgive."

How to retain the decisive quality of the Christian claim, on the one hand, and on the other to affirm the pervasive nature of divine self-revelation and redemption, offers a problem for theologians—one to which they ought to address themselves much more than they have done. But there can be little doubt that the common assumption that Christianity makes such an arrogant claim to complete possession of all the truth, while insisting that nowhere else may men find salvation, not only provides unnecessary offense to those who would find faith, but also negates some of the major emphases in Christianity itself. At any rate, we can say one thing: the imperative for Christian missionary work is not that we shall save from certain damnation those who have not accepted Christianity, but rather that we are ourselves so "lost in wonder, love, and praise" for what God has done for us in Christ, that we cannot rest content until all men have had the opportunity to hear of it and, if God so wills, to share it with us. Ultimate questions of "who is to be saved" rest for their answer in the hands of God alone; and that God is the God who has taught us in Christ that He seeks and saves to the uttermost, and wherever men may have their habitation.

6

The final area to which we must give attention is that of the "miraculous." If by miracle is meant the affirmation that God is not "tied" to His world, that there is a certain open-ness and unpredictability about things, that novel and fresh occurrences may and do take place, then there can be no doubt that miracle is essential to the Christian world view. Nor is there any unnecessary offense offered to men by this affirmation, for despite the apparent regularities and uniformities of life every man is well aware of the fact that there lives "a freshness deep down things," and that the unexpected and unprecedented does occur. But the sort of teaching about miracle that all too frequently is to be heard is quite different from this. It talks of an arbitrary action of God, of demonstration of truth by unnatural wonder, of God intruding Himself into a world from which presumably He has absented Himself since creation. It seeks to prove who Christ is by the assertion that He did miraculous things, that He was born in a way which, to many, renders Him less than human, that He rose from the dead in a way which has no relation to human experience or the rest of our knowledge of the world. It confuses the Incarnation with a virginal conception, and the Resurrection with a reanimation of a physical body. It makes nonsense of the kind of orderly process—orderly even in those unexpected happenings which give that process tang and flavour—which we have every reason to accept as the way in which God in fact works in a world where He is always present, always active, always bringing out of the old things new things that are yet not so much *against* as *more than* that which has gone before.

It is one of the tragedies of our time that some of our most appealing apologists (I think of men like C. S. Lewis) fail to see this and hence, in their presentation of Christian faith, are in danger of confusing essentials with non-essentials, and of making the central affirmations hinge upon what are at best peripheral matters. Often enough these are matters that ought to be investigated by historical science in the light of known facts about the world and about men's thinking concerning that world at particular times and under particular historical circumstances; and in any event they are hardly of crucial importance. Nor are we much helped when we are assured that "the Church has always taught this or that . . ." for on these matters why may not the Church have been wrong, reflecting the thought-forms and patterns of experience known at the time but unable to see through them to the central claims which are the Church's only real *raison d'être?* It is unlikely that those outside the Church, but with access to current writing, will make much sense of any such statement as that "the Church has always taught this," when they know as much as they now do know about the results of biblical criticism and the light that such criticism throws on the way in which man's mythopoeic faculty was at work in biblical times.

7

So much for my three areas. There are many other reasons for the failure of men to respond to the faith, not least being the simple fact that this faith has often appeared to them irrelevant to the life that they must live in the world where they must live it. But of this, as of many of the other reasons, our modern writers have taken due account. What I for one fear is that, even in their insistence on the relevance of the faith and on their ability to show that relevance, many of these writers have forgotten the simple claim of intellectual honesty, the demand for humility before the fact, the need for modesty in all which does not concern a Christian's final commitment, and the generosity of spirit which will welcome new truth because it knows that all truth, wherever found, is God's truth.

It is my conviction, for what it is worth, that the only kind of Christian preaching, teaching, exposition, and defense that will win the men and women of our own time is the kind which declines to make a pretense to absolute knowledge; which gladly makes place in the Christian pattern for all that is good and true; which willingly recognizes the widely diffused work of God, everywhere redeeming men, in various ways and in differing degrees, from frustration, triviality, and shame; which is not afraid to admit mistakes made in the past, even about matters that have been a part, although a peripheral part, of the given tradition; and which, at the same time, is firmly insistent on the central, focal, definitive place of Jesus Christ in the whole relationship of God with man. Some such presentation, in my judgment, will meet modern men and women *where they are.* It will provide for them a faith which is both reasonable and exacting, which asks them to give all of themselves, and which, in return, gives them a peace that passes understanding, but which, at the same time, sends them into the world to live bravely, with conviction and with humility, in the places where they are and with the imperative to labour for the increase of such a measure of charity and righteousness as this world can be brought to express.

8

One final matter deserves some brief attention. Much that we have said in this discussion may meet agreement, insofar as the *intelligentsia* are concerned. "Yes," we may be told, "all that you have been saying has its importance and value, perhaps even its truth, for those who are highly educated and well-informed. But after all, what has this to do with the ordinary man, the simple run-of-the-mill clerk or shopkeeper, the hard-driven housewife, the mechanic, the person who does not read the latest books or keep up with recent developments in science and in philosophy?"

My answer to this hypothetical question is very simple. In the first place I should wish to point out that it is not in fact true that the sort of people who are mentioned are entirely without acquaintance with what is being said and done in the realms of science and philosophy and in other areas of modern advance. The laity are not nearly so stupid in these respects as many clergy seem to assume. With more and more opportunities for adult education; with the wide diffusion of "popularized" science through periodicals that have a circulation in the millions; with cheap reprints of more advanced books as well as simpler presentations of the ideas that are found in them by competent second-hand writers; with the widespread curiosity which brings large numbers of people to listen to, and to read, anything that informs them of the ideas now prevalent in academic circles, we are confronted with a situation very different from the old days when there were a very intelligent few and a thoroughly uninformed many.

But still more important is the simple fact of intellectual honesty. I think that sometimes defenders of traditional ideas do not possess too much of that particular virtue. One has heard ardent support of some specious little book, not on the grounds that the book is adequate as a statement of the faith but simply because the book is easy to read, argues well for the Christian religion, and appears to have been successful in winning a hearing for the Church. Yet surely such an attitude is morally indefensible. We have no right, as apologists for the Christian faith, to use any arguments save those that are as intellectually watertight as we can make them; we have a positive duty to avoid cheap and easy argument and slick turns of phrase that will fool the unwary. It is shocking to anyone who believes that God is Truth to hear a defense of an aspect of Christian truth by an argument which is itself untruthful, or to listen to those who defend, by whatever trick may serve, that which is actually indefensible and which (sad to say) the defender himself probably knows to be indefensible.

Dean Inge once said that the laity have a right to ask but two things of the clergy: "That they shall preach the Gospel and tell the truth." Sometimes one fears that a reason for the suspicion in which we of the clergy are so frequently held by laypeople is precisely that laypeople are not entirely certain that we do "tell the truth."

They have heard enough, outside the church building, of what they have every reason to believe to be actual fact, to preclude their listening with much respect to a parson who seems to wangle his way into a position that is hardly respectable intellectually.

The essentials of the Christian faith, the heart of the Christian message, is indeed intellectually respectable; it is the guarantee of the validity of man's thinking in that it speaks of a Reality who is Himself ultimate reason, as well as perfect value and adorable love. It is quite possible to state the central affirmations of Christianity very simply, yet with complete integrity of mind and with a keen awareness of their relationship to the whole of man's knowledge. That is the task to which we are called in this age of crisis and confusion.

VIII

THE CHRISTIAN TRADITION
AND THE NEW DAY

I<small>N</small> the religious and theological world, the most obvious tendency of the past quarter century has been what
an English writer on religious subjects has styled "the
return to orthodoxy." Nor has this movement been con-
fined to religion and theology; in every area we see its
manifestations—in politics, in social theory, in literary
criticism, as well as in religion and religious thought. In
the contemporary world the term "liberal," used as the
opposite of "orthodox," has come to be a pejorative term.
No theologian, if he values his reputation, dares to call
himself a "liberal," although some hardy souls are willing
to describe themselves as "neo-liberals."

The prevalent school is called "neo-orthodoxy"—a term now used with a great variety of meanings and, therefore, extremely ambiguous, since the confessional theologians who revive the Reformation statements of faith, the "post-liberals" and "post-critical theologians," the defenders of "classical Christianity," are all of them, in one way or another, concerned to "go beyond" the "liberalism" of the late nineteenth and early twentieth centuries; and this "going beyond" very often means "going behind," in the sense of emphasizing the major traditional assertions of Christian faith as found in the Scriptures, in the age of the "Fathers," in the scholastic theologians, or in the reformers of the sixteenth century. We live in the midst of this movement away from what are usually described as the negations, the reductions, the whittlings-away, which it is felt marked the "liberal" era in theology.

Now there is much that is of value in this movement. It is true that there was a tendency, in many areas of the theological world, to minimize and sometimes to dismiss the insights of the historical faith and to seek for a simple theology that could be equated, with some few specifically Christian additions, with the "religion of all good men." Theologians, and many laymen, were willing to describe Christianity as nothing more than the "teaching of Jesus," which they thought to be the affirmation of the Fatherhood of God, the brotherhood of man, high moral and spiritual ideals, with Jesus Himself as the great leader in the human religious pilgrimage. Thus Christ became, at most, a notable prophet, proclaiming religious truths that commended themselves to men because they were in fact what any decent citizen could and would believe. The heights and depths of the Christian revelation were reduced so that nothing was left beyond a vaguely Christian theism, a vaguely Christian ethic, and the use of worship as a kind of dynamo for inspiring men to live according to their best insight and understanding.

I believe that it is correct to say that something like this, with the addition—and it is an important addition —of a keen social awareness and a demanding social imperative, did mark much of what is often described as "liberal Protestantism," at least in Germany, Britain, and the United States. And insofar as this is a fair description of that particular phase in religious thought, we may be grateful that there has been a revolt and thankful that once again the great insistences of historical Christianity—on the reality of the living God, on the sinfulness of man, on the incarnation of God in Christ, on redemption from sin, and the like—have found their central place in the newer theology. "Liberalism," when it was what I have described, had little to commend itself to men and women who know the facts about themselves and their world, and wish to be Christians in some authentic sense of the word.

1

And yet, can we be satisfied with the way things have gone and are going? I, for one, cannot; and the purpose of this book has been to call for another way, to examine the "return to orthodoxy" in a critical spirit, to suggest another mood or attitude as more consonant with the genius of our religion and more likely to make Christianity, in a thoroughly authentic sense, a possibility for our contemporaries. This concluding chapter is an attempt to sum up, to set my position in the light of historical Christian development, and to affirm as vigorously as I can the need for a "new" Christian modernism.

Let me say at once that the word which has been selected to describe the position I advocate is chosen for want of a better one. I am quite aware of the bad connotations of *modernism* for many sincere men and women, as well as for those who are professionally concerned with theology. But in its proper sense, modernism should not be equated with "liberal Protestantism"; it is the word used by Pope Pius X, in his encyclical *Pascendi gregis,* to describe Roman Catholic theologians and writers, both clerical and lay, who sought what one of them, George Tyrrell, described as the belief "in the possibility of a synthesis between the essential truth of [the Christian] religion and the essential truth of modernity." The Anglican Communion was in some ways the natural home of this movement; Professor Sanday, the great Oxford New Testament scholar, came at the end of his life to the modernist view, which he defined as "thinking the thoughts and speaking the language of my own day, and yet at the same time keeping all that is essential in the religion of the past." Members of the other reformed churches also embraced this position—for example, Professor Benjamin W. Bacon, among biblical students, and Dr. Newman Smyth, among theologians. And all of them distinguished carefully between "reducing" Christianity to something else *and* rethinking and restating the Christian tradition, as we have received it, in ways appropriate for the contemporary world.

So, *faute de mieux,* I have chosen the term—more particularly because it seems to me that theologians like Professor Bethune-Baker (whose *The Faith of the Apostles' Creed* I have lately had the privilege of abridging and editing for a popular new edition) have the root of the matter in their approach. If anyone can think of a better word, I for one should be overjoyed; it is not words that count, but the truths which the words seek to state.

2

The position in which Christians find themselves in the world today is a very difficult one. The traditional Christian ideas and the language in which these ideas are expressed seem, to a large number of our contemporaries, without significant meaning for life as they must live it. The same contemporaries, however, are increasingly dissatisfied with a non-theistic humanism, with perfectionist utopianism, and all the rest of the stock-in-trade approaches of a naive progressism. Their basic need, as they themselves increasingly recognize and assert, is for a faith which will give their existence in the world a significance which endures. One finds, for example, a spokesman for moderns like Arthur Koestler, in his recent *Trail of the Dinosaur,* making two affirmations: one, that a religious faith is the only answer to man's dilemma; two, that Christianity is not a faith which can serve men today or which they can serve.

The situation of a man like Koestler cannot be met by a return to classical formulae; it has no contact with a biblicism that is not worked out in language which has meaning for a modern; it finds the ordinary Christian apologetic full of special pleading. Hence Christianity is rejected. It is my conviction that this need not be so. If we are so tied down to the letter of Scripture, to the *ipsissima verba* of traditional theology, and to its unscientific world view which all thinking men (Christians or otherwise) now reject, then no way can be found for proclaiming Christianity save by the use of these outworn images and words. Yet these often convey no meaning to our contemporaries. Hence we must seek to discover the patterns of thought which will in fact communicate the essential meaning behind the scriptural record, the traditional theology, and the philosophical-scientific perspective associated with Christianity. I believe we can do this; this book is, in effect, a preliminary attempt at the task.

3

Nobody who has his eyes open and his mind ready to accept facts, can deny that we are sinners. Nor can he question the obvious truth that sin is not simply individual but is, in some profound sense, racial, so that we are all of us alienated from our true destiny and cut off from the powers which can make our living authentic. But this insight is not inseparably associated with the specific details of the doctrine of the fall of man and original sin, as these are traditionally understood. The possibility and the fact of deliverance in Christ is also a given, which cannot be questioned by those who have experienced it themselves or have seen it in others. But this is not the same thing as saying that any or all of the usual doctrines of Atonement are true. *What we need is to distinguish between the facts and the mode of their statement.* This is a delicate, but it is also a necessary task. It is, in my opinion, the task to which Christian thinkers, in their consideration of man's situation and God's way of dealing with it through Christ, should devote themselves. And this is but one area in theology—and with it, the presentation of the Christian message for our time—which is in need of this sort of radical reconception.

Furthermore, the commonly accepted philosophy of our day, which sees the universe as a graded "system," has such close affinities with much in the basic Christian faith that it provides an admirable vehicle for certain of the specific Christian insights. For example, in such a process, Christians can see the place of Jesus Christ as the focus and crowning manifestation of a movement of Reality, or God, in and through His world. They can also take an attitude towards the non-Christian faiths that is different both from the utter rejection of these by many hyper-orthodox thinkers and also from the too easy acceptance of them by humanists. In these religions there is a preparation for the focus of revelation, Jesus Christ; there is also a real, though partial, disclosure of the Word who in Christ is adequately "en-manned" for our wholeness. So the actual history of religion is, to quote the late Professor C. C. J. Webb, "the story of a single Incarnation of God in humanity, culminating in the life and death of Jesus Christ and in His risen life," whereof the Christian Church is "organ and vehicle." Thus Christianity has the capacity eventually to assimilate and incorporate the whole of man's religious experience, correcting and crowning that which has gone before, or which appears outside, the specific Christian claim.

Or again, the Bible is to be seen in its context in the life of the Christian community, not as an oracular statement of faith and morals—however sophisticated this oracular view may be in our own time and among our new biblicists. The point is that Christianity is based on the faith that is implicit in the experience of new life in communion with God, mediated by the incarnate, crucified, and risen Christ, and imparted to men in the fellowship of the Holy Spirit. So the Bible is to be used, not as a mine for "proof-texts," nor as conclusive and exhaustive in its thought-patterns (varied as they are), but as the testing ground for such development of Christian theology and moral teaching as may occur: the question is whether or not this or that development can be found consistent with the formative picture of Christianity, which is also the normative standard for determining the true nature of the "Christian thing."

4

The attitude which I am here commending is not a new one in the Christian Church. In differing ways, according to different times and places and different historical circumstances, we can see precisely this kind of open-ness, this willingness to rethink and restate, from the days of the Fourth Gospel itself (and even St. Paul) straight through the centuries. As I have indicated earlier, Clement and Origen, in Alexandria; Thomas Aquinas in the middle ages; Baron von Hügel in our own century, provide examples. There has, of course, been a narrower interpretation; some of the great saints have been regrettably obscurantist in their point of view. But the Church has still gone forward, largely through the efforts of those who refused to identify new truth with error.

Failure to recognize this fact and refusal to carry it on in our own time appear to me to be a blasphemous denial of the God of truth and the truth of God, and an unbelieving distrust in the Holy Spirit's guidance, which is promised to the Church of Christ. Our obligation today, then, is to use the traditional formulations not as final statements, not as positions in which we may rest content, but rather as pointers along the path of Christian exploration, with due recognition of imperfections, inaccuracies, overemphases and underemphases, even perhaps of the misleading ideas and implications that may be found in those formulations. It is no awful sin to value these formulations for what they are and for what they accomplished in their own day, while yet seeing their inadequacy for our own. I am unable to understand the mentality of those who believe that, say, patristic definitions of the person of Christ have closed, once for all, the consideration of the meaning of that person; nor can I understand the mentality of those who think that biblical categories as such—and not the meaning which the categories both veil and reveal—will suffice for our need.

On the contrary, the insistence of the Christian ages on the wide cosmic sweep of God's revelation leads me to believe that, in our own time, through biblical study with its critical conclusions, through honest and reverent apprehension of God's ways with men and with His world at large, such as we have been granted through the patient labours of scientists, philosophers, and others in our time, and through every avenue of human experience and reflection, we have been given a deeper understanding of the significance of the Christian Gospel. This we must claim, and this we must establish.

A quarter of a century ago, Dr. Frederick C. Grant, then Dean of Seabury-Western Seminary, put all this in memorable words:

146

A faith so potent through successive ages, so various in its manifestations, so adaptable to changing conditions in generation after generation, so rich in the spiritual illumination of different races and nations of men, has still a secret to unfold in this new age. In fact, one cannot well share the "Catholic" outlook in the twentieth century unless he is something of a "modernist," nor be an ardent "modernist" unless he has caught some glimpse of the meaning of the Catholic faith in the past . . . The great age of the Church is still to come. We are still "in the morning of the times" and the early period of the Church's history is not yet over. Perhaps we in this very generation are among those that stand by, which shall in no wise taste of death, till they see the kingdom of God come with power.[1]

[1] Frederick C. Grant, *New Horizons of Christian Faith* (Milwaukee: Morehouse, 1928), pp. xi and 278. Used by permission of the publisher.

200-1056-C-5